ANTHROPOLOGICAL PAPERS

MUSEUM OF ANTHROPOLOGY, UNIVERSITY OF MICHIGAN

NO. 46

SOCIAL EXCHANGE AND INTERACTION

Edited by
EDWIN N. WILMSEN

Contributions by
ARAM A. YENGOYAN
GEORGE C. FRISON
RICHARD I. FORD
STUART STRUEVER and GAIL L. HOUART
PETER BENEDICT
HENRY T. WRIGHT
CONRAD P. KOTTAK
KENT V. FLANNERY

ANN ARBOR

THE UNIVERSITY OF MICHIGAN, 1972

© 1972 by the Regents of the University of Michigan
The Museum of Anthropology
All rights reserved

ISBN (print): 978-1-949098-09-9
ISBN (ebook): 978-1-951519-24-7

Browse all of our books at
sites.lsa.umich.edu/archaeology-books.

Order our books from the University of Michigan
Press at www.press.umich.edu.

For permissions, questions, or manuscript queries,
contact Museum publications by email at umma-pubs@umich.edu or visit the Museum website at
lsa.umich.edu/ummaa.

CONTENTS

Introduction: The Study of Exchange as Social Interaction
    Edwin N. Wilmsen 1

Ritual and Exchange in Aboriginal Australia: An Adaptive
Interpretation of Male Initiation Rites
    Aram A. Yengoyan 5

The Role of Buffalo Procurement in Post-Altithermal
Populations on the Northwestern Plains
    George C. Frison 11

Barter, Gift, or Violence: An Analysis of Tewa Intertribal
Exchange
    Richard I. Ford 21

An Analysis of the Hopewell Interaction Sphere
    Stuart Struever and Gail L. Houart 47

Itinerant Marketing: An Alternative Strategy
    Peter Benedict 81

A Consideration of Interregional Exchange in Greater
Mesopotamia: 4000-3000 B.C.
    Henry T. Wright 95

A Cultural Adaptive Approach to Malagasy Political Organization
    Conrad P. Kottak 107

Summary Comments: Evolutionary Trends in Social Exchange
and Interaction
    Kent V. Flannery 129

References 137

INTRODUCTION:
THE STUDY OF EXCHANGE AS SOCIAL INTERACTION

Edwin N. Wilmsen

ANTHROPOLOGISTS have long been aware of the interrelations between processes of exchange and the organization of social relations in human societies. At least since the publication of Malinowski's classic, *Argonauts of the Western Pacific* (1922), the exchange of goods and services between independent social groups has been viewed as but one component of a system for regulating interactions between groups. That exchange takes place in the context of social interactions is clear, and the study of the mechanisms through which a balance is maintained between the requirements of the one and of the other has led to an extensive literature, most of which has focused on purely economic issues or upon the forms of economic systems.

The papers in this volume are not concerned with economies as such. Nor are they directly concerned with theoretical issues prevalent in dichotomies such as those represented by the substantive-formalist argument in economic anthropology (see Dalton, 1967, and LeClair and Schneider, 1968, for convenient guides to the literature on this argument) although a substantivist bias is exhibited by all the authors. Rather, the emphasis is on the role of exchange in maintaining and modifying other parts of social systems and on methods by which this role may be examined.

Mauss (1954) has stated as a general principle, and Sahlins (1965) has specified for primitive societies the functional role of exchange in making tangible social ties. Exchange spans the distance between interacting parties; the form of the transaction clarifies the meaning of that distance. Thus, exchange may be looked upon as a form of social communication. All human societies—in common with other animal societies—maintain specific signaling systems through which information about interpersonal and intergroup relational positions is communicated. To the verbal and visual means of conveying the kind and degree of social partitioning between individuals and groups in contact, man has added exchange as a dimension for establishing and

1

maintaining social distance. Exchange introduces an element into the system that is otherwise unavailable; it makes concrete in the present and, more importantly, in the future a relation that signaling systems alone can only announce. A good transferred, a service performed, an agreement to meet again serve to measure the constancy of social distance between reciprocating units when the physical distance between these units varies.

Underlying all transactions are implications of social distance and, as well, spatial components which together specify the nature of exchange interactions. The form of interaction varies as the organizational principles binding participants vary (in simplest terms, as the organizations of hunting bands through national market systems vary). But these forms are united by exchange procedures, which convey information to the participants about their social and spatial positions while reaffirming participant statuses. The context and meaning of exchange are socially specified; similarly, the spatial parameters depend upon more than the situational requirements of the exchange proceeding itself. Goods and services, agreements and obligations, the participating individuals themselves are brought to the point of transaction from different locations within the space allocated to interacting social entities. Exchange distance is, consequently, a variable function of social and physical distance. It is true that participants in an exchange are in some sort of contact—and thus, for the moment, close—but what they exchange and how they carry out the transactions are indicators of their relative positions outside of the transactional situations. Individuals and groups who engage in exchange today may be far apart tomorrow. How and why they move into exchange positions are more interesting questions.

Individuals and societies have variable access to resources, which are themselves unevenly distributed in the environment. Social resources—access to labor, skills and products—are as critical as are natural resources. Exchange networks forge a link between social and natural resources and thus help maintain a balance between social space and environmental space. The study of exchange is but one approach to the larger system of interaction.

The notion that nonsituational information about the organization of social space is contained in exchange procedures is crucial to archaeologists who wish to study the structure of prehistoric social systems. For spatial relations, as corollaries to social relations, provide a means for comprehending their social counterparts when the opportunity for direct observation of social interactions is absent. Descriptive questions—who participates in a situational exchange, to what larger aggregate does he belong, what are the locales of these aggregates, what is exchanged, how far is it carried to the point of transaction and from where—and interpretive questions about the role of exchange in the social fabric are common to the study of exchange systems whether based upon contemporary or prehistoric data. The papers in this volume were brought together to illustrate that common approaches can be found to these common questions.

The spatial and organizational functions of exchange are expressed in almost identical terms by several authors in this volume. Yengoyen argues that the adaptive significance of exchange among Australian bands is that it binds scattered groups into a collective unit that is better able to insure the survival of these local groups than can any one group alone. Exchange underwrites intergroup solidarity in an uncertain environment which can only support small, dispersed population aggregates and creates a larger sphere of social awareness than any single group can maintain. Frison presents a case for direct functional relations between subsistance requirements, group aggregation and exchange mechanisms. He suggests that as an optimum balance between these components is approached, it becomes more economical to form new groups rather than to expand old ones. Near the other end of the organizational scale, Benedict concludes that exchange processes reach beyond specific arenas of transaction and that a major function of exchange systems is to forge a closure between spatially separated activities.

Ford, using ethnographic data, and Struever, using archaeological data, conclude that a significant function of exchange activity is to sustain ritual activities which, in turn, provide the ideological rationale upon which social groups justify themselves. Exchange is thereby seen to play a critical supportive role in maintaining the form of social systems. On the other hand, Wright's work suggests that exchange plays, at best, an ancillary role in modifying social systems, at least at the level of state formation. His data support the conclusion that changes in the political geography of Mesopotamia preceeded changes in exchange volume and trade networks and that population increases stimulated demand for increased traffic in goods and services. Kottak draws similar conclusions from his data.

As is often the case in collections of papers such as this, as many interesting questions are posed as are answered. This is because provocative conclusions stimulate the formulation of even more provocative problems. These papers attempt to study exchange processes as parts of larger systems and, consequently, offer insights into an approach which can incorporate data drawn from both prehistoric and contemporary societies into a search for solutions to common problems.

All of the papers in this volume were read, in preliminary form, during a symposium held on 21 November 1969 as part of the 68th Annual Meeting of the American Anthropological Association in New Orleans. The authors gratefully acknowledge the support of the Wenner-Gren Foundation for Anthropological Research in making this publication possible.

RITUAL AND EXCHANGE IN ABORIGINAL AUSTRALIA: AN ADAPTIVE INTERPRETATION OF MALE INITIATION RITES

Aram A. Yengoyan

ANTHROPOLOGY has always had an interest, overt or covert, in cultural practices which are bizarre, archaic, and usually oriented toward human reproductive functions. In fact, the early founders of the field seem to have been overly concerned with such practices as scarification, totemism, couvade and any form of mutilation of sexual organs. A reading of the journals prior to 1910 indicates that attempts to understand how these practices occurred, their origin and distribution, and their specific cultural content were paramount in most anthropological and antiquarian concerns. With the gradual shift from emphasis on customs to the understanding of society and societal process, the exotic, esoteric and erotic practices became of marginal and tangential interest. In recent times, however, renewed interest in such practices has generated new interpretations. Thus male initiation rituals (e.g., tooth evulsion, circumcision and subincision) among Australian aborigines have provided a means for new theoretical assaults on old problems. The explanations of male initiation rites range from psychological interpretations (Roheim, Bettelheim) to sociological analysis (Radcliffe-Brown) and finally to evolutionary emphasis (Lang). Recently Singer and DeSole (1967) have renewed interest in subincision by proposing the bifid kangaroo penis envy argument. This latter interpretation might be stretched further by suggesting that subincision is another manifestation of the dualism which, according to Levi-Strauss, pervades aboriginal psyche and society.

Subincision and other such rituals may also be interpreted as to their adaptive significance for the maintenance and survival of populations as social units. The problem of how rituals operate and questions of how specific ritual behavior originated must be kept methodologically separate. Origins of such practices will, in all probability, never be fully determined; at most one can only make educated speculations about the dim past.

Nor will functional explanations have any bearing on the question of origins and problems of cultural distribution.

In this paper, my aim is to discuss the adaptive significance of male initiation rites in aboriginal Australia and to offer a possible explanation for the variations in the ethnographic distribution of these practices throughout the continent. A primary purpose of ritual behavior is to promote collective activities between groups and individuals who are socially and spatially dispersed. The combining of groups for ritual behavior promotes population clustering and intergroup interaction as long as the various participating social segments stand in different relationships to one another. Local groups whose ritual contributions to ceremonial activities are qualitatively different from each other will meet with certain nontemporal regularity for the performance of rituals. Ceremonials of nontemporal regularity are significant social mechanisms for combining dispersed local populations for varying periods of time. The duration of these rituals will vary with environmental conditions and the importance of the specific activities. Rituals of this type, where functional specialization and qualitative differentiation among participating groups increase the necessity of ritual performance, are required for the recruitment of adults through age-set specific initiations for males. In the Durkheimian sense, this type of ritual is composed of local groups which are organizationally similar in structure but are functionally differentiated from one another.

A second type of ritual is formed by groups whose interacting social segments are both functionally and structurally similar. Rituals of this type are an ordered set of activities which follow agricultural, religious or political calendars with marked temporal regularity. Agricultural rites among shifting and sedentary cultivators during planting and harvesting would be an example. In such cases, the rituals are time specific in that the particular act occurs with complete regularity as part of the economic, mythological or political structure of the society.

In nonregular, temporally unordered acts like circumcision and subincision, the performance of rituals could only take place under favorable environmental conditions which permitted local groups to cluster for several days. Ample surface waters and an abundance of foods are critical in holding dispersed populations together for varying periods of time. The social organization of these clustered bands was also an important factor in explaining why subincision and circumcision were located in certain areas in Australia and absent in other localities. Assuming for the sake of argument that patrilineal, patrilocal bands were the basis of aboriginal Australian local organization, then the important fact is that the subincisor and circumcisor (i.e., the MoBr) would not have been in the same local group as his sister's son. The sister's son was "cut" by the mother's brother, who in turn was responsible for providing a "daughter" as the future wife of the sister's son. Circumcision and subincision could only occur when two or more local groups had combined for ritual purposes and the exchange of females for marital arrangements. Each band would have been structurally similar, but organic differentiation would have characterized interband relationships. Organic differentiation between local populations in similar ecological conditions is manifest through ritual specialization and cross-cousin marriage, which promotes the necessity of exchanges of acts and females to maintain the viability of the social system. As long as one's subincisor and one's future spouse are in neighboring bands, ritual and cross-cousin marriage tend to increase the solidarity of populations, while ecological factors and a sporadic resource base further the opposite trend—dispersing populations in order to maintain balances in man-land ratios (i.e., population densities).

The spatial distribution of male initiation rites was not uniform throughout Australia. In general, the coastal and interior coastal populations were characterized by an absence of subincision, circumcision or both. However, these rituals were present among the now classic Aranda of the Alice Springs area of central Australia as well as other desert groups such as the Pitjandjara and the Walbiri. Furthermore, these interior groups also had sections or subsections, an elaborate mythological structure and a general cultural complexity which may be interpreted as being "involutional." Tindale's (1940) article and map provide a good distributional account of these practices.

The aboriginal populations of the coastal and interior coastal regions were clustered in tribal groups of small population size occupying relatively limited areas; population densities were about one or two persons per square mile though in specialized environments human densities were probably higher. With access to a terrestrial and a marine biota, high densities are to be expected. As one moves into the interior areas where rainfall averages are less than fifteen inches a year and droughts of major proportions are the rule, the total floral and faunal biomass is exceedingly low. Correspondingly, the overall human population densities were also markedly low. The interior populations were generally larger in tribal sizes, but tribal areas were significantly greater; this resulted in population densities which ranged from one person per 20 square miles to one person per 50 square miles. Curr (1886-1887), Meggitt (1964a, 1964b) and Yengoyan (1968a, 1968b) present more detailed accounts and interpretations of environmental variations and socioeconomic differences.

Variations in tribal sizes and population densities present a number of implications for interband, intertribal and extratribal interaction. In the coastal and interior coastal areas, the relatively high densities among territorially small tribes resulted in local groups which were in close and frequent contact with one another. We have little empirical evidence for the frequency of this interaction, but the early historical accounts from the Sydney area indicate that communication between local groups must have been frequent and rapid, since the aborigines generally knew where the early settlers were and what developments had occurred. Environmental conditions were favorable enough to permit collective activities and meetings for varying periods of time. With ample land and sea foods, the meetings of these populations permitted exchanges and population redistribution. Thus, specific male initiation rites, which were needed to pool populations of scattered local groups in the interior desert areas, were not required as adaptive mechanisms for promoting social intercourse and exchange among the coastal tribes. Furthermore, the coastal peoples were usually characterized by an absence of cross-cousin marriage systems. Local group exogamy along with incest regulations were the major rules governing marriage arrangements. Ecological and demographic factors promoted and maintained frequent contacts between local populations.

As stated earlier, male initiation rites in central Australia brought groups together for ceremonial and marital objectives. With low-density populations in a harsh desert environment, one finds social mechanisms which promote group interaction among spatially diverse groups. Initiation rituals and an elaborate marriage system are thus interpreted as adaptive factors in linking small and scattered groups to each other.

Rituals such as subincision and circumcision, which are noncalendrical and require an organic unity among participating groups for their performance, may be interpreted as adaptive mechanisms which increase solidarity and interaction among local populations. Yet rituals of this type are only one means of maintaining ties among populations which are culturally uniform but spatially dispersed. Populations in harsh environments, which are characterized by spatial and temporal variations in resources, require mechanisms by which all local populations are reciprocally linked to promote interaction and mobility over vast areas of highly limited resources. A genealogical kinship framework does not possess this function since distant relations are kept genealogically distant. However, the Australian section system and the Bushmen name-relationships are other means through which all relations—close or distant—are grouped in a finite number of categories through which linkages with spatially distant kinsmen are determined. A more detailed discussion is presented in Yengoyan (1968*a*, 1968*b*).

In summary, this paper has not attempted to provide an answer to the question, why circumcision or subincision. My argument for ritual groups whose performance requires organic differentiation among participating groups could apply to ceremonial finger nail clipping or the taking of magical hair, as well as penis mutilation. The content of the ritual is secondary to the fact that rituals of this type can only operate when functionally diverse groups are juxtaposed through organic solidarity. It is also hypothesized that societies which inhabit environments composed of poor, limited and sporadic resources require structural devices such as section systems, name-relationships, and organically differentiated ritual organizations through which local populations can expand and contract in order to adjust to varying environmental and social demands.

THE ROLE OF BUFFALO PROCUREMENT IN POST-ALTITHERMAL POPULATIONS ON THE NORTHWESTERN PLAINS

George C. Frison

INTRODUCTION

THIS paper deals with post-Altithermal archaeological evidence from the Powder and Tongue river basins and the adjoining Big Horn Mountain area in north central Wyoming and south central Montana. Postulations on the basis of interpretations from this archaeolgoical evidence are that for about 4000 years of post-Altithermal time, this was an ecological area within which prehistoric groups practiced a hunting and gathering economy that depended strongly on stylized communal means of *Bison bison* procurement carried out at a certain time of the year. These communal procurement techniques were in turn determined strongly by the behavioral tendencies of the bison. Bison were undoubtedly taken whenever possible at all times during the year by individual and small-group hunting techniques, but the large cooperative efforts in the late summer and early fall were a vital factor in providing food for immediate use and, more important, supplies to process and store for use during winter periods when food was difficult and often impossible to obtain. This consolidation of small groups into a larger unit at a predetermined time and place was also a time and means for social, ceremonial and other group activities.

ECOLOGY OF THE AREA

In this area of the northwestern Plains, ecological conditions demonstrate abrupt changes. The Pryor and Big Horn Mountains project first eastward and then southward from the main Rocky Mountains to form a basin between them. This Big Horn Basin is an arid country and reminiscent of the Great Basin country of Utah and Nevada. The Powder and Tongue river country immediately to the east of the Big Horn Mountains receives more rainfall, which is reflected in better grass conditions, and this was buffalo country after Altithermal times. Mountain slopes on the east and west sides produce varied economic resources, both floral and faunal, to elevations above timberline. Apparently the Big Horn Basin was never the scene of large bison herds in post-Altithermal times, but in the Historic period they were forced there by outside pressures. The archaeological record bears this out; communal buffalo procurement sites are common to the Powder River Basin, but they have not been found as yet in the Big Horn Basin.

Almost immediately after the extremely dry Altithermal period, or about 3000 to 2500 B.C., large herds of *Bison bison* returned to the Powder and Tongue river country. Human populations returned at the same time, and either developed communal procurement techniques or, more likely, brought these techniques with them. They probably had only to apply already existing ideas of communal procurement to a slightly different set of topographical and environmental conditions. In addition to the plains, they were exploiting the mountain slopes from foothills to above timberline, and occasionally small groups wandered into the interior areas of the Big Horn Basin. Variations of this cultural pattern probably occurred over much of the northwestern Plains. In considering this cultural system, centered around the bison herds of the open plains, it is important to be aware that there was apparently another, overlapping cultural system, centered in the mountains and mountain-plains border. These ideas have been strengthened by recent explorations in Big Horn Canyon (Husted, 1969:82-97) and in the Shoshone River Canyon (Wedel, Husted and Moss, 1968).

COMMUNAL BUFFALO PROCUREMENT

Part of the hypothesis presented here is that in order to best exploit the *Bison bison* without benefit of horses, it was necessary to limit the large-scale, communal operations to the late summer and/or early fall. Some of the more important reasons for this were: (1) the animals were in best condition at this time; (2) weather conditions were favorable for drying meat and yet cool enough to allow better processing of the carcasses before spoilage could occur; (3) during the spring and most of the summer bison herds contain either young calves or cows in rut, and either or both of these conditions make it difficult, if not impossible, to move the herds without horses; (4) after the rutting season is over, buffalo tend to gather in larger herds, but the large mature bulls congregate into separate herds away from the others. Bulls are a disruptive element in moving a herd in that they continually drop out of the herd and others try to follow. There are other reasons for the timing of these hunts, but these seem of greatest significance.

THE ARCHAEOLOGICAL EVIDENCE FROM THE EARLY MIDDLE PERIOD

Numerous bison traps dating to the immediate post-Altithermal period or about 2000 B.C. are found in the Powder River Basin (Bentzen, 1961; Frison, 1968a). These traps were small, naturally-occurring box canyons of varying size resulting from erosion in alternating hard and soft strata in the bottoms of intermittently-flowing arroyos. Animals were driven into these from the downslope side since for all practical purposes it would be impossible to force bison to jump into a trap of this nature from above. There is some evidence that modifications were made when necessary to hold the animals. This would be difficult to determine, since these traps were located in arroyo bottoms and subject to partial or complete destruction by normal processes of erosion. To date, no complete trap has been found.

Buffalo jumping was also practiced during this time period. On Rosebud Creek in southern Montana, just west of the Tongue River, is unquestionable evidence of buffalo jumping during the beginning post-Altithermal (Frison, 1970). This part of the area contains topographic features favorable for jumping, including perpendicular bluffs with good approaches close to areas of good feed and water. The latter favors consolidation of small numbers of buffalo into larger herds. One hypothesis of buffalo jumping is that a large herd (possibly 100 or more) was a prerequisite to successful jumping. No matter how fast a few head of buffalo are stampeded toward a jump-off, they can avoid it at the last instant. Enough buffalo were necessary so that the momentum of a large, tightly-packed stampeding herd would carry a good share of the leaders over the jump-off. This large herd size was not necessary in the case of trapping, but in a large trap, the manpower requirements are believed to have been about the same as for a jump. Age determinations from teeth eruption schedules indicate these traps and jumps were late summer/early fall operations. Radiocarbon, obsidian, and geological dates range from 2750 to 1500 B.C.

On the basis of typological similarities, the same cultural groups were occupying small camp sites and exploiting a wide variety of foods, both floral and faunal, in the Big Horn Mountains from an elevation of about 6000 feet to above timberline. One dry cave site seems especially relevant (Frison and Huseas, 1968) in that it was a small-group camp, probably a single family, occupied during early and mid summer. Time of year of occupation was determined by the presence of plant foods that mature at this time of the year and which all grow in the area today. A mountain sheep ewe and a young lamb present in the deposits suggest a mid summer kill. A radiocarbon date of 2222 B.C. $\pm$ 150 years indicates the same general period of time as the jumps and traps mentioned above. Numerous other small, open camp sites are indicated by surface material.

The present interpretation from these data is that small single or multifamily groups were widely dispersed during the spring and summer in the mountainous parts of the region. In this way, they were better able to exploit the economic resources. They knew that they would gather with a number of similar groups at one of several alternate locations in the late summer for the purpose of communal buffalo procurement operations. It was necessary to have alternate locations because there was never a guarantee that the buffalo would concentrate in the same part of the region year after year. Winter occupation was probably also in small groups, but at lower elevations. Hunting and gathering was done here but only within a reasonable distance from stored meat processed during the fall operations.

ARCHAEOLOGICAL EVIDENCE FROM THE LATE MIDDLE PERIOD

All of these same hunting and gathering practices continued during the Late Middle period or from about 1500 B.C. to about A.D. 500. Bison jumping continued at the site on Rosebud Creek (Frison, 1970). Small, temporary open sites (e.g., Bentzen, 1963) are found over the entire area. The geology of the area limits most rockshelters suitable for habitation to the mountainous areas, and these indicate summer occupation on the basis of both floral and faunal evidence (e.g., Frison, 1965, 1968b). Evidence for even more sophisticated bison trapping and associated ceremonial activity is suggested by a site in the southeastern Powder River Basin (Frison, 1971) with a radiocarbon date of A.D. 280 $\pm$ 135 years. It is almost entirely man-made, although there were undoubtedly certain features of the immediate area that made it favorable over other similar locations. Subsequent changes due to erosion have made it difficult to perceive these advantages. Main features of this site include two lines of post holes representing a drive lane leading into a trap. A bend in the drive lane obscures the actual trap from the animals until the last possible moment. Anyone familiar with handling cattle knows that they will travel better through a chute of this nature than down a straight lane, and cattle handling techniques can be generalized to include buffalo. The trap itself was indicated by a number of post holes that supported a superstructure of an undetermined nature; it seems unlikely that it was a corral which kept the animals under complete control. During its last period of use, one side of the structure consisted of posts two to three feet apart forming two lines also separated two to three feet. Large logs and brush were probably piled lengthwise between the posts to form an enclosure. With continued peeling of the ground in the kill area, more and more post holes were revealed, leaving a final pattern of post holes which represented several modifications of the structure through time and which obscured much of the exact nature of the structure at any one time. The evidence suggests the animals were shot with large dart points in both the drive lane and the trap itself.

Of perhaps greater interest is what appears to be some sort of ceremonial structure alongside but separate from the trap. This consists of two curved rows of post poles outlining a structure 41 feet long and 20 feet wide vaguely in the shape of a football. One side has thirteen posts the other eleven, and five post holes span the center. Badly decomposed logs are believed to be part of the above ground structure. Around one end of the structure, spaced between the post holes were eight bison skulls, and inside the structure on the same end were three small shallow holes each containing the longest dorsal spine from the hump of a bison. The inside of the structure contained no evidence of habitation; there were no fires, tools, or other items such as are usually found in a habitation structure. There is, however, abundant evidence of camping and meat processing in the areas nearby. The structure in question suggests shamanistic and other ceremonial activities that surround communal food procurement activities in many other contexts. A possible model for the social and ceremonial activity in communal procurement situations is suggested by the interior north Alaskan Eskimo in seasonal caribou kills (Spencer, 1959:353-57). It seems likely that ceremonial activity also accompanied the earlier trapping situations. On the basis of present evidence, there is nothing to suggest any significant changes in cultural activities during these two time periods. There are typological changes, especially in projectile points and to a much lesser extent in tools, but no apparent accompanying functional changes.

ARCHAEOLOGICAL EVIDENCE FROM THE LATE PREHISTORIC PERIOD

Abrupt typological changes in tool and projectile point assemblages do appear with the beginning of the Late Prehistoric period, about A.D. 500. Most noticeable of these is the introduction of the bow and arrow. Unless closer investigations reveal as yet undetected traps, it appears that communal procurement methods in this area became oriented more toward jumping. Late Prehistoric jumps are more recent and consequently better preserved. Preservation is also better due to the face that jumps, unlike the traps, are usually located in places that are not subject to natural destruction.

Although there is evidence of more communal buffalo procurement during the Late Prehistoric period and larger overall populations, there is no evidence to support any significant increase in cultural complexity. There appear to have been more of these separate communal operations occurring, especially toward the end of the period, but there is nothing to suggest that the individual operations were any more sophisticated than earlier ones. There is some evidence to suggest that increased exploitation of the buffalo herds was the result of an influx of peoples from the Missouri River area. Mandan tradition pottery is found in camp areas associated with many of the Late Prehistoric period bison jumps, and this is probably the result of the appearance of the Crow Indians in the Big Horn, Powder and Tongue river basin areas (Frison, 1967a). Crow tradition places the Crow in the area by at least A.D. 1600 (Medicine Crow, 1962a:47), and radiocarbon dates suggest the date may be even earlier (Frison, 1967a:105). Because of better preservation (due mostly to recency of use), much more detail of these operations has been recovered.

Buffalo jumps are necessarily limited to certain locations, determined by the needs of the human group and the behavioral tendencies of the buffalo. The actual jump-off need be nothing more than a clay bank 30 to 50 feet high at a 45 degree or greater angle or a perpendicular bluff no more than 10 to 15 feet high. No matter how lethal the jump-off, the proper conditions of approach are vital to its operation. Behind the jump-off there must be a relatively flat area allowing movement of a herd of sufficient size from the beginning point of the final stampede. Beyond this there must be an area with grass and water to attract and hold the buffalo. As already mentioned, there must be alternative locations to allow for the capricious nature of the animals in collecting in one spot one year and possibly not returning the next. If an otherwise suitable location for jumping buffalo resulted in a large number of dead animals in an inaccessable canyon with no suitable spot for processing the meat, this would not serve the needs of the group either.

Man power requirements placed both minimum and maximum requirements on the size of the human group concerned. At one buffalo jump camp site, there were remains, in the form of stone circles, of twenty known lodges with the possibility of two or three more that were removed. Assuming 6 people per lodge, this would give a total of 120 to 140 people in the group (Frison, 1967b:28). On the basis of handling wild range cattle without horses, I believe that somewhere in the neighborhood of 30 men would be a reasonable requirement for executing a buffalo drive. At least 10 men should be stationed out of sight along each side of the final stampede line, and 10 more would be needed to insure the herd's being brought into proper position. A few more men would add to the probability of success, but beyond this extra personnel would add little to the operation's success; it would be better to form another group to operate in another location.

We can assume also that there were considerable amounts of ceremonial activity associated with these Late Prehistoric period sites, but to date, nothing to compare with the Late Middle period ceremonial structure mentioned above has been recovered. This is not too surprising, considering the large total area involved in a buffalo jump complex and the small portion of this that it is feasible to excavate. Ethnological studies, however, do yield good evidence of ceremonial activity surrounding buffalo jumping and pounding on the northwestern Plains (cf. Shaeffer, 1962:61; Medicine Crow, 1962b:38,41).

In addition to the jumps, small, temporary Late Prehistoric period sites are common throughout the Big Horn Mountains from the foothills to timberline (Frison, 1967a:106-44). Small amounts of ceramics are the key to their cultural affiliations. Some of these (ibid:106-10) are near stone quarries, and the amounts of chipped stone in the camp sites are not commensurate with the cultural activity indicated. It is suggested here that it was a yearly pattern to spend a few days near a stone source in order to make enough tools for the communal buffalo hunt. Supporting this is the fact that in the jump sites and associated processing areas are large numbers of specialized tools, but there is usually a lack of workshop evidence (e.g., Frison, 1967b), suggesting that most tools were brought in ready-made.

One more aspect of bison procurement, policing measures, was important to the society. Bison will remain indefinitely in favorable areas of food and water but do tend to move considerable distances if disturbed. It was necessary to consider group interests over those of the individual since individual hunting might cause the entire herd to move several miles, and there were no means by which to bring them back. Strong central authority was also necessary throughout the process of driving and jumping. These factors and others ultimately served to subordinate the human group to the behavior of the bison herds.

CONCLUSIONS

Bison bison in significant numbers moved into the Powder River Basin and other areas of the northwestern Plains immediately after the alleviation of the severe drought conditions of the Altithermal. They were followed by humans who probably brought with them such techniques of large-scale communal procurement as bison jumps and traps. Both of these utilized natural features of the topography, although varying amounts of modification were needed, especially in trapping situations. The most sophisticated site of this nature found thus far dates from about A.D. 250 and had an associated ceremonial structure.

The time of year, the site locations, and the number of persons involved were all strongly determined by bison behavior. During the Late Prehistoric period, there was a trend away from trapping and a stronger emphasis on jumping. Also during this period, there was an increase in population but not in the complexity of the operations.

This indicates that during a period of about 4000 years the Powder and Tongue river basins and the immediately adjacent area in the mountains to the west presented an ecological area within which prehistoric human populations conducted economic activities dictated largely by bison behavior. During this period, there was little change in the cultural complexity of the groups concerned. They lacked a technology that could offer a serious

BUFFALO PROCUREMENT 19

threat either to the existence of the bison herds or to their normal patterns of behavior. Bison behavioral patterns forced the consolidation of small groups into larger segments at a certain time of the year in a predetermined location. These factors, along with the necessity for leadership during these occasions, strongly affected societal institutions but also kept them relatively unchanged during this 4000 year period. Only when the horse, especially, and other European items, to a lesser extent, became part of the system was there a significant change in Plains Indian culture. The bison herds were totally unable to survive these new innovations.

BARTER, GIFT, OR VIOLENCE: AN ANALYSIS OF TEWA INTERTRIBAL EXCHANGE

Richard I. Ford

I

THE importance of economic transactions between pueblos and between pueblo and nomadic peoples has long been recognized by anthropologists. Archaeologists have documented extensive trade networks involving shells, pottery, precious stones, and other nonperishable items (cf. Schroeder, 1965; DiPeso, 1968). Ethnohistorians have noted exchange of these and other items including hides and meat originating with pedestrian nomads living east of Pecos (cf. Hodge, 1907; Kenner, 1969). Ethnographers have enumerated additional goods exchanged between parties from different tribes. Elsie Clews Parsons (1939:33-37) not only recognized the importance of intercommunity trade but also compiled the most encyclopedic inventory of trade goods to date; however she failed to discuss sustaining mechanisms. One of the earliest southwestern ethnographers, Adolf Bandelier, did recognize three major methods of exchange; the title of this paper was chosen from his work (Bandelier, 1890:39). Nonetheless, from his pioneering efforts to the present, a systematic discussion of the transfer of goods and services has been lacking.

For an area where long distance trade is rooted in antiquity, an in-depth analysis of exchange processes is long overdue. Published sources do not permit this for the entire area, although many unsystematized fragments of evidence are recognizably intriguing. For this reason, an analysis of any single pueblo or group of related pueblos is most useful. As a result of several fortunate circumstances, I was able to begin research on Tewa exchange systems in 1962, and my interest has been sustained while I have been conducting ethnobotanical investigations in New Mexico. When this study began, several elderly pueblo consultants had actually engaged, as children, in trade expeditions at the beginning of this century, and all knew tales about trading episodes that can be corroborated by historical documentation. Although quantitative data is not available, thus limiting the analysis, enough information was obtained at San Juan, Santa Clara, and San Ildefonso to reveal the outlines of this complex activity. Published data derived from the remaining Tewa villages is less systematic but nevertheless supports the conclusion that the emerging generalizations apply to all Tewa pueblos. Thus this paper will detail the types and more importantly the bases of exchange engaged in by Tewa pueblos among themselves, with other pueblos, and with nomadic societies.

II

Extracommunity trade is no simple matter in areas lacking a unifying hegemony. Beyond the protective limits of the community, stranger becomes trespasser no matter what his purpose may be. Lacking protection, trade must insure itself; that is, the security of the traders becomes a paramount rule of the game, not the hardness of the bargain or the exactness of the deal. Rates of exchange then, take on little meaning in a marketing sense when distance traveled, relative need, and even survival are part of the calculation.

To understand why trade flourishes under such tenuous circumstances, we must view it as an essential feature of a regional system. Any region consists of unevenly distributed natural resources, climatic variables with a differential impact, and a number of communities with varying population sizes and political organizations. Broadly defined, exchange becomes the major link among these communities.

Material items change hands between members of groups occupying different territories for a variety of reasons. The most obvious is that one group has access to a particular raw material which is unavailable to others. Unequal access may develop when neighboring groups are adapted to different ecosystems, resulting in complementary emphasis on different resources or material goods. There is also a stimulus to trade when, despite living in similar ecosystems with comparable quantities of raw materials, one community emphasizes certain craft objects while another accentuates these artificial differences by specializing in different crafts. In this instance, both could very easily produce the same goods.

The transfer of services and service personnel between communities parallels material goods but also exhibits several important differences. Two communities may have different institutions as a result of dissimilar adaptations and therefore be dependent upon each other for a critical service. Several forms of intervillage cooperation arise when one group may borrow, buy, or in some way obtain a particular service institution from another group. Subsequent to the purchase or loan, they may maintain contact for purposes of initiating new members into the organization or of sharing symbolic localities possessed by one of the parties. Another form relates to demographic differences that may exist or arise between communities. Such variability may result from random, microdemographic changes concomitant with a small population base or from demographic catastrophes caused by disease, warfare, or emigration. Regardless of the precise reason, personnel from one community are used by another in positions that would normally be occupied by members of the latter if it had an adequate population base.

Social relations and sacred requirements are also determinants of exchange. As Sahlins (1965) has argued, cost accounting the price of goods varies along a social dimension. A relative is given advantages denied to strangers, but even strangers of high status often must behave like kinsman to validate their position. Even belligerence between neighbors can be viewed as a form of exchange when the result, among other goals, is the procurement of goods, including land, or services, including slaves. The stronger the social polity, the greater the role the government has in intercommunity economic affairs. However, if the societies have weak polities, then we expect that the prevalence of a strong ritual system and the need for esoteric goods to support it will generate exchange.

A Tewa-centric regional system is a perfect laboratory for studying these general propositions. The participating societies exhibit a number of adaptations; the goods and services vary from one sphere to another; and the types of exchange are equally as variable.

III

The Tewa are a self-defined linguistic group composed of six pueblos—San Juan, Santa Clara, San Ildefonso, Pojoaque, Nambé, and Tesuque—located in north central New Mexico along the Rio Grande and several of its tributaries (Fig. 1). These communities have been visited and studied by anthropologists for a number of years (e.g., Harrington, 1916; Parsons, 1929), but it is only through the more recent work of Dozier (1960, 1961, 1970) and Ortiz (1965, 1969) that we are beginning to understand the underlying tenets of Tewa ritual structure and world view.

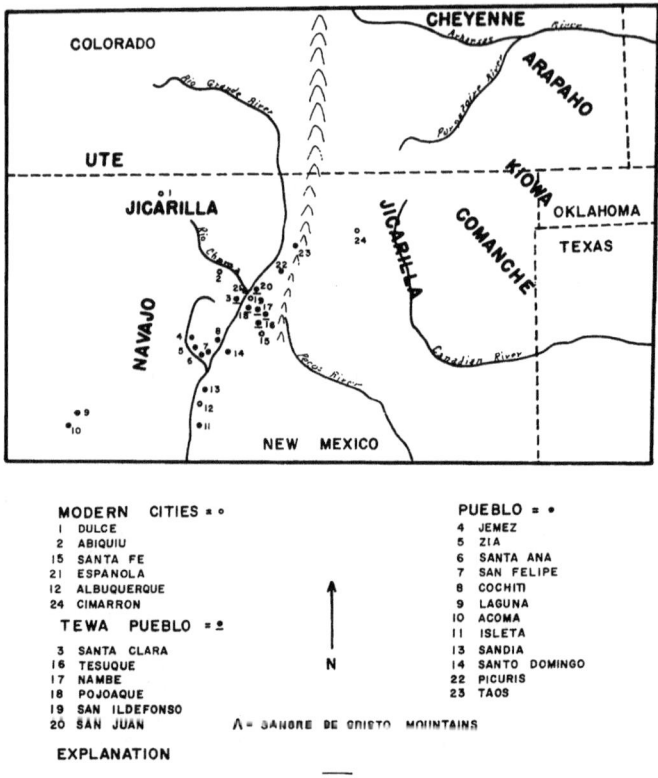

Fig. 1. Societies engaging in Tewa intertribal exchange.

The local ecosystems vary slightly from pueblo to pueblo, but basically they are similar. During the period under consideration, the nineteenth century and first decade of the twentieth, individual village populations never exceeded 400 residents. The subsistence economy was based on the irrigated production of native corn, beans, squash, and kitchen garden crops as well as on gathered greens, roots, seeds, and fruits. Hunting contributed significantly to the diet during the winter when deer and elk were hunted locally, while early fall hunting expeditions to the plains of eastern New Mexico brought back antelope and buffalo meat.

Tewa food and craft production is embedded in the household which is often extended to include several generations. However, the vagaries of the Rio Grande environment are such that no matter how many hands may be available or how much land one may have inherited from his bilateral relations, natural disasters often limit productivity and result in both an unpredictably differential food supply for each family and a meager surplus for the village as a whole. Production variability of craft objects has a different basis. Craft items are not manufactured in every household. Some families make very few items, relying instead on bartering or borrowing for their needs. At the other extreme are the families in which one or more members produce a surplus intended for external consumption. Excepting ritual activities, most economic affairs are not coordinated by anyone except the household itself.

At a higher level, each Tewa pueblo is organized into two dual divisions and several cross-cutting sodalities. For ritual and other purposes the head (cacique) of each moiety has ceremonial custodianship over the community for part of the year. With few exceptions, all members of the community belong to their father's moiety, and each cacique is assisted by a sodality composed of his own moiety's members. These moiety-based sodalities and the other associations organize dances and rituals of a specific nature and perform other explicit functions. The Bear curing societies, the Kossa and Kwirena clown societies, and the Hunt society have an obligation to assure the well-being of people, plants, and animals. The Scalp society, a warrior sodality, is linked to the Women's society which helps with the care of the scalps. It is through sodalities that all dances are performed and the symbols appropriate to each steadfastly maintained.

Facing the outside world are other organizations with political and protective functions. The most conspicuous person is a Spanish-imposed and American government-recognized governor who is selected annually. He has other assistants, but his decisions must be seconded by a village council. The other organization consists of the war captains, a native institution modified by Spanish authorities to assist them against other Indians, who are also appointed on an annual basis. They have the twofold task of defending the pueblo from outside attack as well as protecting all persons participating in rituals, public and secret.

In a weak, diffuse polity with a low, differential household production, the ritual system helps to regulate many of the ecological variables of each Tewa ecosystem, and trade becomes a necessary safety valve for pueblo survival. But since each Tewa pueblo was part of a larger state hegemony—Spanish, Mexican, and American—which was unable to adequately protect individual pueblos, still less the traders going between communities, until the end of the last century, we begin to understand something about the difficulty of trade. The acuteness of this problem is evident in an examination of Tewa commerce with Plains Indians.

IV

While sedentary villages exaggerate their ecological differences for the advantages of exchange, such dissimilarities naturally existed between the Tewa pueblos and Plains equestrian nomads. The former were potentially self-sufficient with their dependency upon farming, gathering from highly productive plant communities, and hunting. The nomadic hunter was not so fortunate. His dietary mainstay, meat from the chase supplemented by gathered plants with unreliable yields, forced the Plains hunter to fulfill his nutritional needs by maintaining contact with villages like the pueblos which, on the surface, appear not to have needed him.

Under these circumstances, one could posit that the advantage during trade transactions was with the pueblos, but this was not the case. Most of the time the mounted nomad held the advantage of surprise. If needed commodities were not in ample supply, the nomad entered the Rio Grande Valley and took his chances on pillaging the requisite amounts. Even if unsuccessful, his efforts still caused havoc and destruction. Warfare is normally a very inefficient means for procuring necessities; on the other hand, the risk of losing everything with nothing in return by refusing to trade is also a foolhardy strategy. Need and security, two dimensions of a dynamic interaction, compelled economic cooperation.

COMANCHE

The above is far from an empty theoretical statement, for it describes one facet of the relations between the Tewa and the Comanche. But an unanswered question remains: why did the Tewa bother to undertake the dangerous and risky venture out to the High Plains in eastern New Mexico, western Texas, and southeastern Colorado to hunt and to trade with the Comanche? The answer lies in their social milieu and the changes in the local ecosystems of each Tewa pueblo as a result of Hispanic colonialism. Farming and commitment to sheep and goat herding in the hills and lower mountain slopes of the Rio Grande Valley north of Santa Fe changed the resource base of the pueblos. The resulting cleared land for crops and pasturage led to a reduction in the number of deer and elk readily accessible to each village, and consequently a decline in meat for winter consumption and hides for trade, two traditional economic commodities for which the Tewa were noted. Game was still available in the mountains to the west, but as will be discussed later, the presence of Navajo marauders severely curtailed economic exploits in that direction. At the same time, the Tewa needed ceremonial objects and other specialty goods which the Keresan pueblos supplied in exchange for hides and leather goods. Thus the Tewa, who were not totally committed to the trade with nomads in the 1700's, certainly came to rely on it in the next century.

For their part, the Comanche shared a social environment with the Tewa but acted within it in a quite different way. They could and did raid and rob Spanish rancherías the same as they did the pueblos. But when it came to amiable exchange with these villages, their options were not limited to the Tewa. Comanche bands also could trade with the Tiwa at Taos and Picuris, the Towa residing at Pecos, or the Keres. Lacking firm trade partnerships, they were under no standing obligation to any one village or group of pueblos. After examining eighteenth century documents, Adams and Chavez (1956:112) concluded "whether they are at peace or at war, the Comanches carry off all they want, by purchase in peace by theft in war." And Bandelier, who in the 1880's was closer to these events, summarized the situation in a way that sounds like a paraphrase of elderly Tewa consultants' sentiments about the Comanche:

The latter [nomads] could "never be trusted"; they might trade peaceably to-day, and murder to-morrow those with whom they bartered. The Pueblos had always to be on the *gui vive* (Bandelier, 1890:164-65).

Parsons (1939:1030) also noted this trade today and raid tomorrow tactic of the nomads. When the Comanche arrived at a Tewa pueblo there was trade; the stakes were too high not to trade, even when surpluses were almost nonexistant. The Tewa aim was to stave off plundering at any cost. Contrariwise, there were times when the Tewa did need certain provisions from the Comanche, who, if they did not come into the valley that year, had to be sought out despite the risks such journeys entailed.

Tewa-Comanche exchanges took place at three different localities: at the Taos trade fairs, in Comanche camps on the High Plains east of the Rockies, and outside the individual pueblos. Despite the locality, many aspects of the trade—goods, time of year, and personnel—were similar, but the all important guarantees to peace of trade highlight the differences.

The Comanche desired above all else wheat bread, cornmeal, and other agricultural products such as dried apples and melons. Occasionally they requested pottery, metal tools (especially knives), cotton blankets, and turquoise. For their part the Tewa needed mostly dried buffalo meat and prepared hides. Comanche horses were also obtained by bartering, and it was through the Comanche trade that the pueblos got wooden bows made of osage orange (*Maclura pomifera*) which grew in Oklahoma and Texas and walnuts (*Juglans nigra*), another eastern product. As previously hypothesized, it was more than pure economic need and gain that maintained this trade. It was from the Comanche that the Tewa obtained most of their bison heads, needed as ritual paraphernalia for dances, and special bison neck hair which was also of ritual importance.

The Tewa, naturally enough, preferred to trade in the early fall after the harvest was in, and this was the usual time. But this did not militate against their participating in the Taos fairs in July and August or going to the Plains at other times if they survived the winter with a surplus.

While all Comanche males had access to Tewa traders, the same was not true for the Tewa. Tewa trade expeditions were composed of about six to twenty men who had something to exchange or who had a desire to go. They, in turn, would also carry the produce of fellow villagers. These traders could be from one village or, as was often the case, from several pueblos. Leadership was ephemeral and fell to individuals who knew the area to be traversed and who could speak some Comanche. During the last century, several individuals from San Juan and Tesuque were noted for this ability. Spanish apparently also served as the *lingua franca* as it did for interpueblo exchange.

Spanish civil authorities policed the Taos fairs where settlers, traders from Chihuahua, and Indians assembled to barter their wares. Despite precautions, brawling occurred, and even after a successful fair the Comanche sometimes proceeded down the Rio Grande, continuing to trade at one pueblo while raiding the next. In 1774, the Comanche stole Nambé's horses; four days later they arrived at the Taos fair where they sold 140 animals. In the same year they attacked Santa Clara and San Juan, gaining no horses but killing three men (Thomas, 1940:169-72). At times Spanish authorities attempted to keep the Comanche from attending the fairs (Bancroft, 1889:249). But such efforts were rather transparent since both parties depended on goods or the return of captives from each other.

Outnumbered and vulnerable without the important element of surprise, the Comanche were at the mercy of the ruthless Chihuahua merchants' inflated prices and had their goods and animals stolen by the local settlers, whose actions prompted the government to guard the Comanche camp (Thomas, 1940:31). This spirited situation was vividly captured in 1776 by Dominguez:

> When they [Comanches] are on their good behavior, or at peace, they enter Taos to trade. At this fair they sell buffalo hides, "white elkskins," horses, mules, buffalo meat, pagan Indians (of both sexes, children and adults) whom they capture from other nations. They also sell good guns, pistols, powder, balls, tobacco, hatchets, and some vessels of yellow tin (some large, others small) shaped like the crown of the friars' hats, but the difference is that the top of the hat is the bottom of the vessel. ... They acquire these articles, from the guns to the vessels, from the Jumanas Indians (Wichitas), who have direct communication and trade with the French, from whom they buy them. The Comanches usually sell to our people at this rate: a buffalo hide for a *belduque,* or broad knife made entirely of iron which they call a trading knife here; "white elkskin" (it is the same hide, but softened like deerskin), the same; for a very poor bridle, two buffalo skins or a vessel like those mentioned; the meat for maize or corn flour; an Indian slave, according to the individual, because if it is an Indian girl from twelve to twenty years old, two good horses and some trifles in addition, such as a short cloak, a horse cloth, a red lapel are given; or a she-mule and a scarlet cover, or other things are given for her.
> If the slave is male, he is worth less and the amount is arranged in the manner described. If they sell a she-mule, either a cover or a short cloak or a good horse is given; if they sell a horse, a poor bridle, but garnished with red ranges, is given for it; if they sell a pistol, its price is a bridle; if both together, a horse is given for them. This is the usual, and a prudent judgement of how everything must go can be based on it. They are great traders, for as soon as they buy anything, they usually sell exactly what they bought; and usually they keep losing, the occasion when they gain being very rare, because our people ordinarily play infamous tricks on them. In short, the trading day resembles a secondhand market in Mexico, the way people mill about (Adams and Chavez, 1956:252).

As noted above it was often as a consequence of these fairs that Comanche bands visited the pueblos, although they did come at other times. The frequency of these visits is unknown.

Going to the Plains was often high adventure for the Tewa. Such expeditions followed the harvest and the transfer to Winter Moiety leadership of the pueblo (Ortiz, 1969). These parties, which combined buffalo hunting with trading, faced a two-fold difficulty. The first was locating the Comanche, and the second was avoiding belligerent Plains Indians with whom most of the Tewa did not trade.

Tewa traders lacked trade partnerships with the Comanche. The explanation for this was 1) the problem of finding any appropriate band, much less your partner; 2) the failure of most Tewa to trade every year; and 3) the stresses inherent in the not infrequent hostilities that arose between the groups. Consequently, Tewa traders were dependent upon the good will of the band leaders for hospitality and protection. Trading commenced with a gift from the Tewa to the Comanche leader, usually an item which was in short supply that year. Each group had its own encampment, but meals were taken in the Comanche camp upon invitation. Nevertheless, the possibility of chicanery was present, and the Tewa always went in pairs to their host's lodge. After the exchanges were concluded, the nomad leader would give the Tewa expedition leader a departing gift which usually unbalanced the exchange. This gift might be a horse, several highly prized osage orange bows, or prepared bison heads to be used in the Tewa buffalo and game dances.

With peace of trade guaranteed by the Comanche band leader, the Tewa still had to return to their villages, hopefully unmolested enroute. Although Santa Clara Pueblo did have some exchange with the Kiowa (Dozier, personal communication), the other pueblos did not and on several occasions skirmished with them. It fell to the Comanche to swing the balance of power to the Tewa, who were poor in arms and men, by siding with them and even going so far as to escort them to the safety of the Sangre de Cristo Mountains if it were known that Kiowa bands were in the vicinity. The Tewa were not always so fortunate. In San Juan today one can hear about an ill-fated expedition which lost all its stock when it was attacked by Kiowas. (Bandelier recorded this much of the event from a Cochiti informant in 1880; see Lange and Riley, 1966:162).

> They fought the Kiowas and sent them "running like ants" after they shot their leader with an arrow. A band of Comanches were met as the pueblo Indians were slowly heading home. The Comanches gave them horses, buffalo meat and hides, and a feast, and provided protection to New Mexico. San Juan gave them what cornmeal, flour, and bread they had.
> Two years later San Juan traders accompanied by a Mexican Comanchero returned dressed in Santo Domingo style with their hair in bangs and cues instead of braids. Again Kiowa encountered but did not molest them. Their disguise fooled them until one impatient man from San Juan noticed his pony which had been stolen at the time of their initial rout was being ridden by a Kiowa and demanded its return. The Kiowas were now prepared to fight, but some Comanches, who had accompanied the San Juan Indians, said that, if the Kiowas fought the men from San Juan, they must fight the Comanches, too. The Kiowas retreated leaving the Comanches and the San Juan Indians to trade and to feast. This time they had plenty of goods and exchanged corn, cornmeal, wheat flour and bread for buffalo hides and meat and horses.

After 1850, depredations against American ranching interests in Texas caused the newly instituted American civil authorities in the Territory of New Mexico to attempt to stiffle Mexican and Indian trade with the Comanche. A permit system, instituted to reduce trade, had little effect on the Pueblos. Calhoun's correspondence reflects the typical lenient attitude of these administrators:

> The Pueblo Indians are in the constant habit of trading with the Comanches, which ought to be <u>gently</u> <u>and</u> <u>quietly</u> <u>stopped</u>. In every instance I have promptly given to these applicants a simple permit, without charging a fee of any amount, but treating them with the greatest <u>kindness</u> and <u>hospitality</u>, the latter at some <u>considerable</u> <u>cost</u> ... (Abel, 1915:106)

This was just as well, for these agents used knowledge of the location and intentions of the Comanche in eastern New Mexico which they derived from Tewa traders (Abel, 1913).

The Comanche trade did not die easily, especially since a sack of wheat bread would secure, for the Santa Clara trade at least, a highly esteemed Comanche pony (Parsons, 1939:34), and the demand for meat and hides supplied by the Tewa to other pueblos remained strong.

The Comanche trade continued until at least 1874. Agent Pope in 1872 reported that this trade "is virtually stopped" (Pope, 1872:303), but in 1874 Agent Lewis reported that eight Pueblo Indians were killed returning from trading with Comanche (Lewis, 1874:309). Later that year, the Comanche were neutralized in Palo Duro Canyon and removed to their reservations.

UTE

Trade with the Ute bands had many parallels to the Comanche trade, but the decisive element of coercion was missing. Ute forays were generally directed against Spanish settlers and Taos and Picuris Pueblos. Unless Utes were contacted at trade fairs, trade was conducted in the fall and by small groups of Tewa men led by a man with knowledge of southern Colorado, Ute etiquette, and the rudiments of Ute language, although Spanish and sign language were freely used by both parties. Like the Comanche and other hunting peoples, the Ute required nutritional supplements from sedentary farmers, but the amount is unknown. The Tewa recognized this and felt that they always came out ahead in any transactions since the Ute needed their corn, wheat flour, and bread more than they did Ute deer and antelope meat and hides. Prior to their being forced onto reservations in western Colorado in the late 1880's, the Ute were contacted in the San Luis Valley or just over the mountains to the east. For their part, the Ute could also meet Tewa traders at Española fairs or at Abiquiu when they came to receive U.S. government commodities. Utes also visited the pueblos of Santa Clara and San Ildefonso, but these visitations were irregular and never became formalized into trade partnerships. This conclusion is reinforced by the fact that the Tewa do not distinguish the various Ute bands with whom they traded.

The goods again represented the products of their respective adaptations. Buffalo, deer, and antelope meat and hides, horses, backed bows, beaded vests and leggings, and Navajo blankets (for which the Ute were middle men) were sought. In return, the Tewa provided the much needed cornmeal, wheat flour, and bread as well as dried fruit, tobacco (*Nicotiana rustica*), sugar, and coffee. Additionally, Santa Clarons brought pottery and San Juan traders supplied pottery and woven goods. Again, ritual goods were not excluded, as Ute traders were the only source for red ocher paint used in the deer and war dances, among other winter rituals, and a blue dye, also of ceremonial importance. And a consultant at Nambé maintains that their Serpent Dance was "bought" from the Ute by traders.

Certain aspects of the Ute trade are remembered in more detail by San Juan and Santa Clara consultants than are details of the Comanche trade, although they surely apply to both. Each Tewa trader rode either a horse or a burro and lead one or two produce laden burros. To prevent spoilage, the wheat bread was oven baked to a biscuit-like hardness and the cornmeal was parched for an extra long time. Large willow wicker baskets were used to transport the goods. The flour was placed at the bottom with the bread above, and the pottery and woven goods were tied to the top of the load.

Since this trade involved gift giving and bartering, exchange rates are difficult to ascertain. A basket load of flour or bread would bring a hide or a bundle of dried meat. These mainstays had an almost fixed rate, but the other goods varied considerably. Sometimes the red ocher was bartered for while at other times it was given as a departing gift. Horses were usually gifts, but this was a change from 1776 when Frey Dominguez saw Utes trading at an Abiquiu fair. At that time, the Ute needed horses and were willing to give fifteen or twenty deerskins for a single horse. Deer and buffalo meat were also exchanged for corn or corn flour. One deerskin would bring two iron knives (Adams and Chavez, 1956:252-53).

In the eighteenth and first two-thirds of the nineteenth centuries, the amount of trade with the Ute varied greatly. But with the termination of the Navajo threat and the waning of the buffalo (and a consequent end of trade with the now reservationized Comanche), Ute trade witnessed a short-lived renaissance at the end of the last century, only to slowly expire at the beginning of this century.

JICARILLA APACHE

While it may have been difficult to locate the Comanche and Ute on their nomadic rounds, such was not the case with the more sedentary Jicarilla Apache living on their rancherias in the Cimmaron area of eastern New Mexico. When they took up residence in the mountainous valleys north of Abiquiu in the nineteenth century, their commitment to both bison and deer hunting helped keep this trade alive. Even with the near extinction of the bison and the passing of Plains nomadism, the Jicarilla continued to hunt while they adopted herding. Both pursuits distinguished them ecologically from the Tewa and served as a basis for trade up to the present.

With the Navajo menace gone, the environment of each Tewa pueblo further degraded, and the Ute farther away than the Jicarilla, exchange between the Tewa and the Apache intensified.

We do not know when the strong trade ties between the Tewa, particularly San Juan Pueblo, and the Apache began; but by the end of the last century, they had developed classic trade partnerships, with partners being inherited within families through three generations. When a San Juan man, with or without his family, arrived in Jicarilla territory, he went directly to the encampment of his trade partner and presented him with a gift, usually consisting of farm produce. Families were expected to come to the mid-September fiesta at Dulce to which they brought (and still bring) fresh crops. For their part, the Jicarilla were welcome anytime at the houses of their partners in San Juan. Bringing their families, they usually came with gifts of meat or hides for the San Juan saint's day (June 24) and at Christmas time. Each was given shelter, sustenance, and security when in the village of his partner. As one might expect with an arrangement of this type, culmination of a transaction might be delayed for a period of a year or more since, as the San Juan villagers state it, "We are friends, almost relatives."

The Tewa provided the Jicarilla with the same products as

were traded to the Ute and Comanche, with the important addition of birds. It was through San Juan trade partners that the Jicarilla obtained song birds and feathers for certain ceremonies. The Tewa received hides, meat, horses, goats, leather goods, and coiled baskets which they used for domestic purposes and in the Basket Dance and other ceremonies. Santa Clara and San Ildefonso villages also obtained oregano (*Monarda menthaefolia*) and osha (*Ligusticum porteri*), an important medicinal plant and charm.

With the Jicarilla-Tewa trade, too, there were people who were conversant at a rudimentary level in the other's language. In this case, although the observation is impressionistic at best, more Tewa spoke Apache than Comanche or Ute, simply because more people were involved and contacts were made several times a year.

V

Tewa economic relations with the Navajo were another matter. As if the unfriendly incursions of Plains nomads making their forays into the Rio Grande valley from the north or south at the expense of the Tewa pueblos were not enough, there was a peskier and seemingly ever present predator to the west. But as a result of this antagonistic social interaction, we witness yet another type of Tewa exchange.

Prior to their ill-fated incarceration at Bosque Redondo, the Navajo were the primary enemy of the Tewa. Although the full historical documentation of the events is incomplete, the evidence is ample to verify many of the tales about Navajo warfare that are well-codified in Tewa folklore and inculcated upon youngsters even today. History says: "several Indians from Iledefonso [sic] came to me [Agent Calhoun] yesterday also, saying the Navajos were impudent, troublesome, and dangerous—and that they were in every nook and corner of the country" (Abel, 1915: 42). Legends state that people were not safe away from the protection afforded by the village. Venturing to one's field was particularly dangerous at harvest time, as the Navajo were prone to surprise the unwary, taking his crops or driving off his stock.

However, once the pueblo was alerted to the danger, the war captains led volunteers from one and sometimes more pueblos in pursuit of the provocateurs. A successful encounter meant not only death to one or more of the plunderers and the return of stolen property, which was secured by young teenage boys who accompanied war parties, but also the opportunity to plunder the

possessions of the Navajo victims. The all important scalps
would help bring blessings to the community; Navajo ponies
brought esteem to the owner; and silver, turquoise, coral, and
jet were valued by all.

Upon returning to a Tewa pueblo, warriors redistributed
stolen property to the rightful owners, and as the student of the
pueblos would expect, the warriors and their booty underwent a
four day purification rite. The scalps became the property of
the Scalp society to be cared for, fed, and propitiated for the
benefit of the pueblo. After the rites, the other property became the possession of the person who took it. Of these items,
coral and jet were highly prized as charms used in ceremonies
and carried by individuals for protection against witches.

Sahlins (1965:148) calls this type of economic transaction
negative reciprocity—something for nothing. Needless to say,
the success of each Tewa war party could not be assured and
dependence upon this type of economic activity for necessities
would be risky, if not foolhardy. Unlike many ceremonial items,
these were durable goods which accumulated in the society rather
than being destroyed in the course of rituals. It is not that the
Tewa eschewed warfare; they did not, and their reputations attest to
this fact. But while revenge is sweet, the consequent rites could
be an inconvenience. One could even hypothesize that the very
consequences of successful raids were socially detrimental and
a deterrent to more frequent offensive activities. Even though
the Tewa procured most of their jet and a substantial portion of
their coral through warfare with the Navajos, engagement followed
provocation. At this time, Tewa war efforts were retaliatory.

After 1870 this pattern disappeared, and Tewa and Navajo
traded directly at various pueblo fiestas, especially at Jemez.

VI

One senses the drama of Tewa exchange with nomadic tribesmen: the burros slowly wending to the east with the villagers
left behind being well aware of the dangers lying ahead beyond
the sacred peaks of the Sangre de Cristo Mountains, the traditional eastern edge of the Tewa world; or the family, perched
on horseback or nestled among the trade goods in a wagon,
anxious to reach Dulce in time for the Jicarilla San Antonio Day
fiesta; or the successful traders, returning from the Comanche
or Ute, dressed in their newly acquired beaded clothing and
singing as they circled the pueblo four times to "rub off the foot-

steps of their journey." These moments were missing from interpueblo exchange. The amount of goods was less; contacts, informal and infrequent, were usually between individuals rather than large contingents; and craft products, personal services, and ceremonial items replaced food as the major exchange items supplied by the Tewa.

The movement of goods between pueblos proceeded in three ways. The most common was, and continues to be, through individual itinerant traders visiting a community to barter or sell goods or through friends visiting after the harvest. The second took place in the trading atmosphere which prevailed during saint's day fiestas at these pueblos; the last was an exchange of ceremonial goods which accompanied the lending of ceremonial services by ritual personnel.

In these exchanges the Tewa provided a wide variety of goods and services to their nearest non-Tewa pueblo neighbors. A glance at Tables 1 and 2 quickly reveals that San Juan and Picuris, Santa Clara and Jemez, and Tesuque and Cochiti had more complex exchange networks than did the others. Each Tewa pueblo was delighted to barter its crafts, and all were able to provide their common specialty, hides and leather goods which the Tewa prepared themselves or transferred in their roles as middlemen between the northern pueblos and nomads and the southern pueblos.

Many young people are "on the hoof" or "thumbing" today, but itinerant traders from Santo Domingo have been ahead of them for more than a century of recorded history (cf. Whipple *In*: White, 1935:19). Within the 1960's some have made their way to Chicago simply to peddle their fine turquoise and silver jewelry. On a more regular basis, individual traders are known to go door to door in the Tewa pueblos, again specializing in jewelry or ceremonial items like parrot feathers, shells, or woven goods obtained by them from the Zuñi, Navajo, or Hopi.

While some pueblos like Santo Domingo have a tradition of specialization in certain crafts, other specialties have evolved in the present century as the environment and pueblo life styles have changed. As an example of the latter situation, several women from Jemez Pueblo now visit the Tewa villages to sell paper bread and tomales—once part of the daily diet but now replaced by packaged and convenience foods—and plant medicines and charms like *cachana* (*Liatris punctata*). Picuris Pueblo still trades its well-known micaceous cooking ware, but it also has developed a new niche—selling wild plant products used ritually in other pueblos.

At Picuris all the residents will gather plant medicines, especially osha and contrayerba (*Kallstroemia californica* var. *brachystylis*), wild tobacco (*Nicotina attenuata*), ritual brooms (*Bouteloua curtipendula*), and charms like tishasi (*Monarda comata*) for their friends and affines in the Tewa pueblos, but for more than half a century one man from here has walked and hitchhiked, blanket tied around his waist and braids draped carelessly over his shoulders, to peddle his herbs at the saint's day fiestas up and down the Rio Grande valley. In the Tewa villages his arrival is anticipated, and after feeding him in their home, those desiring his herbs will transact for them. This role that Picuris has held throughout this century illustrates but one way sedentary villages specialize to facilitate trade and how the pueblos are linked by a need for sacred symbols and, as we shall see, ritual personnel in order to properly execute their pueblo way of life.

Material goods are payment for ritual services. Persons from Picuris and Taos come with hides, meat, wheat, oats, corn, or pottery to San Juan to pay for a cure by the Bear Medicine society. The Bear from Santa Clara have a close relationship, including initiations, with the Jemez Bears (Lange, 1959:259). When members of these sodalities share services, the host provides food and goods, often comprised of ceremonial paraphernalia which may be otherwise difficult to obtain. Tesuque curers go to Cochiti for their initiation with a similar appropriate exchange taking place and the Kwirana from both pueblos assist each other upon invitation. Cochiti Kwerana also have ties with Nambé and San Ildefonso (Lange, 1959:350). Although these interpueblo exchanges of services are infrequent, nonetheless they provide a means for the distribution of certain types of expendable ritual materials like feathers and dancing gear which by other means are very expensive or difficult to procure.

Some years Tewa men would go in the fall to saline lakes in Estancia Valley southeast of Albuquerque to obtain salt; but if times of turmoil prevented their leaving, salt could be bartered from Isleta or Laguna traders at the Santa Ana or Santa Domingo saint's days. Men from these pueblos were also a source of macaw and parrot feathers.

Under the cloak of peace many other traders attended the saint's days in the pueblos. These participants were not limited to Indians since Spanish-Americans and Anglos to this day avail themselves of the convenience these occasions afford to obtain a variety of goods.

When belligerence prevented traders from Tewa pueblos from reaching pueblos to the west, other parties served as mid-

TABLE 1.
GOODS AND SERVICES PROVIDED BY THE TEWA PUEBLOS TO EACH OTHER AND TO OTHER SOCIETIES

	San Juan	Santa Clara	San Ildefonso	Nambé	Tesuque	Cochiti	Santo Domingo	Laguna
San Juan		food woven goods wicker baskets pottery hides Kossa midwife	food woven goods wicker baskets hides Kossa midwife	food pottery woven goods hides Kossa	food pottery woven goods hides wicker baskets	hides leather goods meat pottery	hides leather goods meat	hides leather meat
Santa Clara	food drums rattles pottery Kossa		food pottery rattles drums Kossa	food pottery rattles drums Kossa	food pottery rattles drums Kossa	hides leather goods meat pottery	hides leather goods meat	hides leather meat
San Ildefonso	food pottery Kossa	food Kossa		food pottery Kossa	food pottery Kossa	hides leather goods meat pottery	hides leather goods meat	hides leather meat
Nambé	food pottery mica Kossa	food pottery mica Kossa	food pottery mica Kossa		food pottery mica Kossa	food pottery Kossa	hides meat	hides leather meat
Tesuque	food feathers turquoise	food feathers turquoise	food feathers Kwirana	food feathers turquoise cacique Kossa Kwirana medicine men midwife		food hides medicine men Kwirana Kossa	hides leather goods meat	hides leather meat

TABLE 2.
GOODS AND SERVICES PROVIDED BY OTHER SOCIETIES TO THE TEWA PUEBLO

	Cochiti	Santo Domingo	Laguna	Isleta	Jemez	Picu
San Juan	drums turquoise silver Hopi mantas feathers	turquoise silver feathers shells Hopi mantas Navajo blankets	salt feathers	salt feathers	twilled baskets specialty foods cachana	pottery wheat hides wild p
Santa Clara	drums turquoise silver Hopi mantas feathers	turquoise silver feathers shells Hopi mantas Navajo blankets pipe dance	salt feathers	salt feathers	food twilled baskets specialty foods hides cachana medicine men	pottery wheat hides wild p
San Ildefonso	turquoise feathers silver Kwirana	turquoise silver feathers shells Hopi mantas Navajo blankets	salt feathers	salt feathers turquoise	twilled baskets specialty foods cachana	pottery hides wheat wild p
Nambé	food drums feathers Kwirana	turquoise silver feathers shells Hopi mantas Navajo blankets	salt feathers	salt feathers	twilled baskets specialty foods cachana	hides wild p
Tesuque	food drums feathers turquoise medicine men Kwirana Kossa	turquoise silver feathers shells Hopi mantas Navajo blankets	salt feathers shells	salt feathers	twilled baskets specialty foods cachana	hides wild p

Table 1. (continued)

Isleta	Jemez	Picuris	Taos	Jicarilla Apache	Ute	Comanche	Navajo	
hides leather goods meat	leather goods meat pottery	vegetables corn chili pottery woven goods wicker baskets curing	pottery food woven goods curing	corn wheat vegetables fruit wicker baskets birds	corn wheat fruit tobacco sugar coffee pottery woven goods	corn wheat fruit woven goods tobacco pottery	corn wheat pottery	San Juan
hides leather goods meat	food leather goods pottery rattles medicine men	food pottery rattles	food pottery rattles	corn wheat vegetables fruit	corn wheat fruit tobacco sugar coffee pottery	corn wheat fruit tobacco	corn wheat pottery	Santa Clara
hides leather goods meat	food leather goods pottery	food	food	corn wheat vegetables fruit	corn wheat fruit tobacco	corn wheat fruit tobacco	corn wheat	San Ildefonso
hides leather goods meat	food leather goods	food	food	corn wheat vegetables fruit	corn wheat fruit tobacco	corn wheat fruit tobacco	corn wheat	Nambé
hides leather goods meat	food leather goods	food	food	corn wheat vegetables fruit	corn wheat fruit tobacco	corn wheat fruit tobacco	corn wheat	Tesuque

Table 2. (continued)

Taos	Jicarilla Apache	Ute	Comanche	Navajo	
wheat oats hides pottery buffalo heads	meat goats horses coiled baskets hides beaded clothing leather goods	meat hides horses beaded clothing red ocher blue dye Navajo blankets bows	buffalo: meat, hides horses bows clothing buffalo: hair, heads walnuts	meat horses blankets jet coral	San Juan
wheat oats hides pottery buffalo heads	meat goats horses coiled baskets hides beaded clothing leather goods osha oregano	meat hides horses beaded clothing red ocher blue dye Navajo blankets bows	buffalo: meat, hides horses bows clothing buffalo: hair, heads walnuts sophora beans	meat horses blankets jet coral silver	Santa Clara
hides buffalo heads pottery	meat goats horses coiled baskets hides beaded clothing leather goods osha oregano basket dance	meat hides horses beaded clothing red ocher blue dye Navajo blankets bows	buffalo: meat, hides horses bows clothing buffalo: hair, heads walnuts	meat horses blankets jet coral silver	San Ildefonso
hides buffalo heads	meat hides animals coiled baskets beaded clothing leather goods	meat hides horses beaded clothing red ocher Navajo blankets serpent dance	buffalo: meat, hides horses bows clothing buffalo: hair, heads walnuts	meat horses blankets jet coral	Nambé
hides	meat hides animals coiled baskets beaded clothing leather goods	meat hides horses beaded clothing red ocher Navajo blankets	buffalo: meat, hides horses bows clothing buffalo: hair, heads walnuts	meat horses blankets jet coral	Tesuque

dle men and continued in this role even after the threat was gone. Traders from Santo Domingo brought from Zuñi shells which originated in the Gulf of California and feathers of Mexican origin to the Rio Grande. Santo Domingo and later Cochita traders obtained dance kilts and woven mantas from Hopi for eventual trade to other pueblos including the Tewa, while Navajo blankets and horses could be obtained indirectly from Jemez or Ute traders. With the termination of any threat to Tewa traders going westward, some Tewa traders did venture to Hopi and Zuñi, but the majority of the goods from these pueblos continued to come through the Keresan middlemen.

VII

Within the Tewa pueblos some commerce was based upon some villages specializing in certain craft products. San Juan was noted for its woven blankets, willow wicker baskets, and pottery; Santa Clara also manufactured a particular type of pottery as well as drums and gourd rattles; San Ildefonso also had pottery for exchange; and Nambé made cooking ware.

Food stuffs were involved in intra-Tewa exchange but were negotiated for by individuals. In no instance was there regular movement of food from one village to another. Need was predicated on losses caused by environmental fickleness or by unexpected expenditures of surpluses. Transactions for food could take place at any time of the year, with relatives in other pueblos often the first to be approached.

Another type of specialization must not be overlooked. Tesuque and San Juan had midwives who were visited or summoned by persons from other pueblos, especially if a difficult birth was expected. Women from San Ildefonso and Santa Clara used the services of the San Juan midwives while Pojoaque and Nambé women went to similar specialists in Tesuque.

To understand the movement of ritual goods from one Tewa pueblo to another and the sharing of ceremonial specialists, we need to examine briefly the demographic situation in these communities. Various epidemics starting in the late eighteenth century and culminating just fifty years ago left the populations at very low levels (Table 3). Some persons were left with no potential mate in the local pueblo and the pueblo itself was left without certain religious leaders. Faced with a preference for village endogamy and a rule to marry no closer than a fourth cousin, a person from a depopulated pueblo had no alternative except to marry someone from outside, preferably a Tewa speaker from another pueblo. This in turn established a network of affines with whom goods could be exchanged or borrowed with returns in both cases delayed until a later date. The loss of ceremonial personnel had long term implications, too. One documented example exemplifying the pattern occurred in 1914 when the Nambé Summer moiety's cacique died without leaving a replacement. In this case the Tesuque cacique filled the role until he had completed the training of two replacements (Curtis, 1926: 66). The Winter moieties of these same pueblos also cooperate as do the Bear Medicine societies (Parsons, 1929:115, 123). In addition, at other times the Kwirana from Tesuque participated in ceremonies at San Ildefonso while Kossa from Santa Clara, San Juan, Nambé, and San Ildefonso have combined forces in each of these pueblos.

TABLE 3
POPULATION OF TEWA PUEBLOS IN THE PAST

Pueblo	Year					
	1760	1860	1890	1905	1930	1968
San Juan	316	341	406	425	530	1277
Santa Clara	257	179	225	325	382	769
San Ildefonso	484	154	148	250	123	305
Pojoaque	99	37	20	—	7	75
Nambé	204	103	79	100	129	266
Tesuque	232	97	91	100	120	230

Note: Reference to Dozier (1970:122) except for 1890 entry which is Donaldson (1893).

As a reward for their assistance, sodality members from other pueblos are given food, "presents," and other items that the host pueblo suspects they need, the latter often consisting of sacred medicines, charms, feathers, or other ceremonial paraphernalia.

We have noted in discussing Tewa trade with other tribes that the ritual needs of the pueblos were one stimulus to trade. This was not unrelated to economic exchange between Tewa villages themselves or changes in population size. The red ocher obtained from the Ute is used in the Deer Dance and various war associated dances. If a pueblo needed more than it had for the performance, as was the case in Santa Clara at the turn of the century, members of the sodality sponsoring the dance approached their counterparts in another pueblo to borrow the needed material. At the earliest appropriate opportunity, however, a trading expedition went to the Ute to obtain this material along with other items. Following the Santa Clara expedition, San Juan was repaid in kind for its loan.

Costuming for dances posed another problem. It was appropriate for each family to own the necessary costumes to enable its members to be full ritual participants. But many of the items deemed proper ritual apparel actually come from outside the Tewa area. For example, in the Tablita Dances men wore shell bandoliers from the California coast and the women black mantas often from Hopi and jewelry from Santo Domingo. In the Buffalo Dance, the bison heads were secured from the Comanche, or more recently from Taos, and the abalone shell pendants came from Santo Domingo or Cochiti but ultimately from the West Coast. The men in the San Juan Turtle Dance wore Hopi dance kilts, Plains beaded arm bands, and parrot feathers from Mexico derived from Keresan traders. If a family lacked these or many other items that could be enumerated, they would attempt to borrow them from fellow villagers; if unsuccessful, they would get them from relatives or friends in other Tewa pueblos. Eventually, a family would have to use its infrequent surpluses to purchase the needed items. The problem has been more acute since the turn of the century when the Tewa populations started to increase again (Table 3). Larger family sizes have generated more borrowing and great pressure to trade for ceremonial items. Recent demographic changes may have accelerated the trade in these goods, but the same underlying incentive to engage in intra-Tewa and intertribal commerce has always existed.

VIII

The Spanish fairs, which brought together Plains and Pueblo Indians, came to an end as trade across the Santa Fe trail increased. At first this change had little impact on the Tewa or their Spanish neighbors, but eventually peddlers, often German immigrants, started to contact these people. And in 1863 the first sign fortelling the future came with the establishment of a merchantile store in San Juan Pueblo. Here manufactured goods could be bartered for in the traditional manner or purchased with currency. Spanish Americans brought their produce to the Tewa pueblos at almost any time or in concert with others on saint's days. While Indian pueblos often specialized in the production of particular craft goods, Hispanic villages rarely adopted this pattern; individuals specialized in the sale of goods like goatmilk cheese, firewood, or carvings, but their competition could be a fellow villager or persons from other towns.

Exchange of services was part of the Spanish-Anglo-Tewa economic sphere. Tewa worked on ranches and in other ways contributed labor to a colonial economy. However, what is not widely known is that medicinal information was shared by Tewa medicine men and Spanish curers. Tewa Bear men in San Juan frequently obtained herbs from *curanderos* in Chamita and Alcalde, neighboring Hispanic towns. These contacts also involved discussions of potions but not the actual curing rituals themselves.

IX

The record of Tewa exchange remains incomplete. This paper has described the major items involved in intertribal trade and has discussed the mechanisms and conditions which sustain commerce. Nevertheless, information is inadequate for some Tewa pueblos and may even be irrecoverable. Furthermore, the missing quantitative information prohibits an in-depth analysis of the dynamic processes which are truly the foundation of commerce. Be that as it may, the data, as fragmentary as they are, do support our earlier theoretical statements and give us ideas to examine in another place and at another time.

Regional trade is a form of foreign policy. Each society interacts on different terms, but it is this social atmosphere, and not the goods themselves, which determines the form of bartering, gift giving, or violence. The Comanche and Kiowa could offer the Tewa the same goods, yet one was a sometime friend and the other a constant foe.

The social environment constitutes one determinant of trade, but the adaptation of the respective parties is another. The subsistence differences that distinguish nomadic from pueblo life point to food as a major trade commodity. While craft objects were always part of the transactions, foodstuffs were paramount. Quite the opposite characterized the relations between Tewa and southern pueblos. These groups had similar subsistence and technological bases. Consequently, we find craft items and services exchanged more often than food. Infrequently, corn, wheat, and other foods were exchanged in some quantity, but this was at times of crop failure. Picuris and Taos, then, were not as anomalous as Table 1 would suggest. Their locations at higher elevations away from the Rio Grande resulted in frequent crop losses and even an inability to cultivate chili and other kitchen crops. Thus, food was often as important to them as to the nomads.

By contrasting the adaptations of the trading communities, we can also see differences in the relative social statuses of those consumating a deal. The band leader of the Plains Indian tribes was the man with the most prestige. Pueblo ritual heads rarely ventured into dangerous areas so far from the pueblo. The Plains Big-Man's (Sahlins, 1968:88) generosity was all that stood between success and disaster for Pueblo traders. He feted the visitors, gave the parting gifts, and assured a safe return. In the arena of interpueblo trade, social relations were important. Affines and relatives in other pueblos were comparable to Jicarilla trade partners, with an imbalance and delay of payment not uncommon. However, this was not so when services were rendered. On these occasions the sodality heads would meet and payment in food and goods was given immediately after the ritual was completed. This stricture applied to cures; the Taos or Picuris family paid what they could regardless of the final outcome. Midwives received their rewards under the same circumstances.

While adaptation determined the nature of exchange and social relations structured it, ritual required it. Parrot and macaw feathers, bison hair, turquoise, and red paint, derived from foreign exchange, were continuously expended in ceremonies. Only trade could replenish the exhausted supplies. All trade items were not consumed in the ritual cycle, but as we have seen, costume requirements changed directly with population pressure. More people generated more trade for ceremonial accouterments. The pueblos lacking Big-Men or chiefs (Sahlins, 1963) who used sumptuary goods to validate their status, used ritual demands to perpetuate trade relationships. Nevertheless, trade with gaily dressed Plains Indians led to an influx of beaded moccasins, shirts, vests, and leggings and created a crisis. Wearing these daily was not cause for concern but donning them in rituals was a serious breach of custom. The solution was not to ban them entirely, but until recently they were not to be worn in Kiva ceremonies or in dances considered ancient by each Tewa pueblo. Interestingly enough, only items obtained from southern pueblos— feathers, shells, dance kilts, and mantas—could be worn in these rituals. But in the face of new contacts and ever increasing exotic goods, the religious organization "gave" to absorb the new while maintaining the old. Thus, dances that the Tewa considered introduced could be costumed with items from nomadic societies.

However, we must not interpret exchange for ritual goods as the only basis for exchange. For all parties, the constant demand for expendable sacred items maintained a valuable linkage between populations that, in the case of the pueblos, tended toward closed, self-sustaining systems or, in the case of nomads, gravitated toward alternative means and markets. Once anthropologists rid themselves of the notion that corn, beans, and squash gave sedentary southwestern Indians a lifetime of security, the necessity for these links can be understood. In times of famine when other regulatory mechanisms proved inadequate, contacts, perpetuated by ritual needs, gave the pueblos access to the produce of other ecosystems.

Warfare was the source of several goods with sacred significance. However, their use as a personal charm did not require a constant supply. Unlike other ceremonial items these were not removed from circulation except when the owner died. In the period covered in this paper, the Tewa were not aggressive combatants; they protected their property but were not in need of booty for their existence.

Today, the study of Pueblo exchange is rapidly becoming the domain of archaeologists. Hopefully, studies such as this one will convince archaeologists that simply knowing the distribution of limited raw materials will explain neither how trade is conducted nor why it is maintained. By ignoring demography, social structure, ritual, and the social milieu, the prehistorian cannot possibly understand trade or, worse yet, advance beyond the meager discussions now available.

AN ANALYSIS OF THE HOPEWELL INTERACTION SPHERE

Stuart Struever and Gail L. Houart

INTRODUCTION

THE fine arts or antiquarian orientation of archaeology in the nineteenth and early twentieth centuries focused attention on the highly visible earthworks of the "ancient mound builders." In many cases these turned out to be Middle Woodland period sites. These earthworks, almost exclusively associated with ritual and burial activity, yielded a specific range of aesthetically pleasing artifacts that were observed to be stylistically similar in scattered Middle Woodland manifestations in Ohio, Illinois, Michigan, Wisconsin and elsewhere.

With the systematizing of archaeology in the twentieth century, and with its focus upon a qualitative, nonstructural, stylistic description of culture, these artifacts became the diagnostic traits of a unitary "Hopewell Culture" that stretched from New York to Kansas, from Michigan to Florida. While regional differences within Hopewell were recognized in passing, these were never defined nor did they beome the basis for asking historic or processual questions. A single, inclusive Hopewell Culture remained the operational unit in treatment of the research problems of the day, though much energy was directed to determining the specific place of origin of the trait complexes that characterized the various Hopewell regional expressions.

With the development of new questions in archaeology, focusing on delineation of prehistoric cultural systems and the attempt to explain variability in these systems through time and space, intensive regional archaeological programs developed that sought to excavate the full range of site types that included the by-then-famous centers associated with the Hopewell Culture in Ohio and elsewhere. As part of this new orientation in archaeology, habitation sites were excavated which, along with diagnostic Hopewell Culture artifacts, yielded culinary pottery and projectile point styles that appeared to be associated, not so much with a single, widespread Hopewell Culture defined in terms of a few status-related artifacts, as with a number of yet undefined local Middle Woodland adaptive systems.

As the intensive investigation of Middle Woodland living sites increased, together with a focus on the complete range of those artifacts, features and food remains which reflected local ecological adaptations, it became abundantly clear that a unitary Hopewell Culture was a phenomenon of archaeological sampling error. This resulted in the first place from a fascination with the archaeological remains of ceremonial-mortuary behavior (and associated fine art) which disclosed many between-region similarities in the grave goods recovered from Hopewell mounds. A unitary Hopewell Culture was also, however, the construct of a widely held "normative" definition of culture. The latter concept, the aim of which is to define a prehistoric culture in terms of the material goods that reflect the mental templates of the participants, largely ignored both the systemic and adaptational characteristics of culture. The increased realization of the importance of the latter concepts to an understanding of prehistoric cultural variation changed the strategy of Middle Woodland site excavation. Subsequently, it also produced data disclosing marked regional variability in a number of Middle Woodland complexes which had disclosed those artifact forms on which the original definition of a unitary Hopewell Culture was based.

DEFINITION OF THE HOPEWELL INTERACTION SPHERE

Against this background, the suggestion was made that what had been treated as regional developments of a Hopewell Culture represented instead different culture types between which some form of interaction existed (Caldwell, 1964; Winters, 1964; Struever, 1964). The raw materials and artifact forms most frequently shared by these Middle Woodland expressions included copper earspools, celts, and breastplates; chipped obsidian artifacts; marine shell containers; worked bear teeth; cut mica sheets and silhouettes; plain and effigy platform pipes; human figurines and a special class of pottery described as "Hopewell ware." It was hypothesized that selected local Middle Woodland groups in eastern North America obtained these items by participation in a series of transactional systems for which the term *Hopewell Interaction Sphere* was coined.

The specific mechanisms responsible for movement of goods (and ideas) in the Interaction Sphere remain to be delineated.

Formal comparison of Hopewell artifacts in the various participating localities showed that unaltered raw materials and stylistic concepts, as well as finished goods, were moving through the networks. Certain general conformities in burial practices suggest the interaction also involved the dissemination of ideological rationalizations for use of these goods. It is also clear that considerable local reinterpretation of diagnostic Hopewell artifact forms and ideological concepts occurred.

Diagnostic Hopewell artifacts appear to have functioned primarily in the social subsystem of the regional Middle Woodland cultures. Their form and context indicate that possession of these artifacts was status-restricted; certain items may have functioned to communicate status, while others served as paraphernalia in the ritual reinforcement of status.

While the final disposition of Hopewell artifacts was often in status graves, most do not appear to have been made specifically for burial furniture, nor were the local Middle Woodland expressions in which they appeared part of a burial cult spanning much of eastern North America. Recent investigations in habitation sites in the Scioto and Illinois valleys (Prufer and others, 1965; Rackerby, 1969) indicate diagnostic Hopewell artifacts were kept and used in the community, where they were frequently lost. Instead of mortuary items per se, they appear to have been status-specific objects which functioned in various ritual and social contexts (including burial) within community life.

Significantly, artifacts associated with subsistence activities (specifically, projectile points and storage and cooking pottery) differ stylistically between regional expressions that share in common the diagnostic Hopewell artifact forms. Styles in these subsistence-related artifacts serve to define the four southern Great Lakes Middle Woodland regional traditions outlined in an earlier paper (Struever, 1965). By the same token, not all local expressions in the Havana, Crab Orchard and other traditions yield Hopewell artifacts. It is believed that continued research will enable definition of local complexes that lack Hopewell Interaction Sphere artifacts, while they share culinary pottery and projectile point styles with various neighboring localities that, in contrast, do yield diagnostic Hopewell artifacts.

In sum, it is hypothesized here that a distinction exists between the Middle Woodland regional traditions and Hopewell. Representing contemporaneous archaeological expressions in the Great Lakes-Riverine area, each is defined on the basis of a different functional category of artifacts. Whereas a regional tradition is defined by styles within artifact classes belonging to the subsistence technologies, artifact types diagnostic of Hopewell functioned in the social subsystem where they served integrational or social maintenance tasks. This helps to explain why a local Middle Woodland group could share certain artifact styles (or "types") with other groups over a large geographic area—the basis for defining a tradition—while simultaneously lacking artifact types belonging to a second and entirely different functional category possessed by some, but not all groups within a tradition. Instead, styles in this second functional category were shared by specific local or regional groups in many traditions, all of whom participated in a series of transactional systems of different kinds and on different scales. For example, Scioto tradition groups located in the Scioto River-Paint Creek area of south-central Ohio shared Hopewell artifact styles with Havana tradition groups concentrated in the Illinois Valley, with Crab Orchard groups located at the mouth of the Big Muddy River, with groups of an undefined tradition centered in the Kansas City area of the Missouri Valley and so on.

Archaeologically, then, this Hopewell Interaction Sphere cross-cuts a number of Middle Woodland traditions and manifests itself in restricted areas of each. Certain exotic raw materials, artifact styles and modes of burial ceremonialism serve to define the Hopewell phase of Woodland culture history of the various traditions in participating localities only.

The failure at the present time to go beyond this simple description of the Hopewell Interaction Sphere reflects: a) the lack of careful analysis of the kinds and distributions of exotic raw materials and artifact styles within and between the participating cultural units, and b) the tendency to accept Prufer's (1961; 1964) Ohio Hopewell chronology which places the six major, intensively excavated Ohio centers into three different time periods.

It is possible to argue that Prufer's Ohio Middle Woodland chronology is not based upon either stratigraphic or radiocarbon evidence, but upon the logical argument that formal trait similarities and differences between sites specifically reflect temporal relationships. In his words,

It seems eminently reasonable that those sites which show the strongest connections with Adena are most closely related to that culture complex while those which show few resemblances are not. If, moreover, some of the latter sites show connections with, or foreshadow traits common in or typical of, post-Hopewell culture units, these sites might legitimately be considered to represent a late phase of the Hopewell Complex.

Accordingly, by noting the differential distribution among the six
Ohio centers of "submound features such as crematory basins,
burial platforms, log cribs, stone cist tombs, 'charnel houses',
etc." along with "Adena-like ceramics (Scioto Ware) and classic
Hopewell pottery, the presence or absence of tubular pipes, and
cruciform gorgets," Prufer places Tremper and Mound City into
"Early Hopewell," Seip, Harness and Hopewell into "Middle
Hopewell" and Turner into the "Late Hopewell" period (Prufer,
1964:49).

The difficulty with this trait comparison is that it represents
a univariant approach to explaining similarities and differences
between cultural expressions; i.e., it fails to consider factors
other than change or continuity in time to account for variability.
Therefore, the preponderance of cremations at Tremper and
Mound City is thought to reflect earlier Adena practices, while
inhumation at Turner reflects a "later" burial mode. In fact,
the distribution of cremations and inhumations may reflect
sociological differences between individuals or groups interred
at large, regional mortuary centers (Hopewell and Turner) on
the one hand, and those buried at small, local centers (Tremper)
on the other.

If the early date (335 B.C.) based on a composite shell
sample from Hopewell Mound 25 is omitted as unreliable, the
two dates from the Hopewell site (94 and 1 B.C.) and one each
from Tremper (100 B.C.) and Seip (A.D. 55) suggest contemporaneity, albeit on slim evidence. In turn, all three sites fall
within the bracketing dates of the apparently long occupations at
Russell Brown (Harness Group) and Mound City. There is
nothing in the radiocarbon dates from the five large Ohio centers
that allows them to be aligned in a temporal sequence; on the
contrary, the dates argue for contemporaneous occupations at
all five, though some occupations may have begun earlier or
lasted longer than others.

In sum, the writers are reluctant to accept the assumption
that formal trait similarities and differences between sites
specifically reflect temporal relationships, and therefore logical
style continuity is not a firm basis for chronology building within Ohio Middle Woodland. In addition, the radiocarbon evidence
enables us to treat the six large Ohio centers as, in part, contemporaneous. The fact that various of these centers share a
number of specific, complex art forms (e.g., mica geometric
figures) which probably had a limited temporal span corroborates
this interpretation of contemporaneity and allows us to consider

the relationship between these centers within an interaction rather than a chronological sequence model.

DEFINITION OF REGIONAL TRANSACTION CENTERS

It is possible to recognize clear structural differentiation of sites within most of the Middle Woodland regional expressions in the Great Lakes-Riverine area. Therefore, the Ohio "Hopewell" centers are not only more complex as a group than the sites of other contemporary groups participating in the Hopewell Interaction Sphere, but certain among the Ohio centers stand out for their size, complexity of earth constructions, and quantity and diversity of Interaction Sphere products.

Seven, and perhaps as many as twelve, Middle Woodland sites in the Great Lakes-Riverine area, spaced between 40 and 180 miles apart and located for the most part on major navigable rivers, fit the above description and may be termed *regional transaction centers* (Fig. 1). Their size and complexity in each case sets them apart from the remainder of the regional population of Middle Woodland sites to which they belong. Trempealeau, Albany, Ogden-Fettie, Golden Eagle, Twenhafel, Mann, Hopewell and possibly five other sites in the Great Lakes-Riverine area share the fact that they are larger, more internally complex, and often yield a significantly greater quantity of Interaction Sphere goods than the remaining Middle Woodland sites in their particular region.

The northernmost of these transaction centers is the Trempealeau complex of mound groups,[1] located in the upper Mississippi Valley in west-central Wisconsin. The cluster of 6 mound groups in the Trempealeau complex encompasses approximately 36 acres and includes 113 mounds (McKern, 1931). Though all these mounds are not demonstrably Middle Woodland, most of those that have been excavated are. One hundred and sixty miles downstream from Trempealeau on the Mississippi River lies the Albany complex which includes about 96 mounds (Pratt, 1876; Tiffany, 1876; Nickerson, 1912). One hundred miles south of Albany in the central Illinois Valley lies the Ogden-Fettie site with its 35 mounds and single geometric earthwork covering ca. 65 acres (Cole and Deuel, 1937; Hesselberth, 1945; 1946). Ninety miles downstream from Ogden-Fettie, at the mouth of the

---

[1] The Trempealeau complex consists of two mound group clusters. One cluster includes the Shrake I, Shrake II and Trowbridge mound groups; the second cluster includes the Schwert, Second Lake and Nicholls mound groups.

HOPEWELL INTERACTION SPHERE ANALYSIS 53

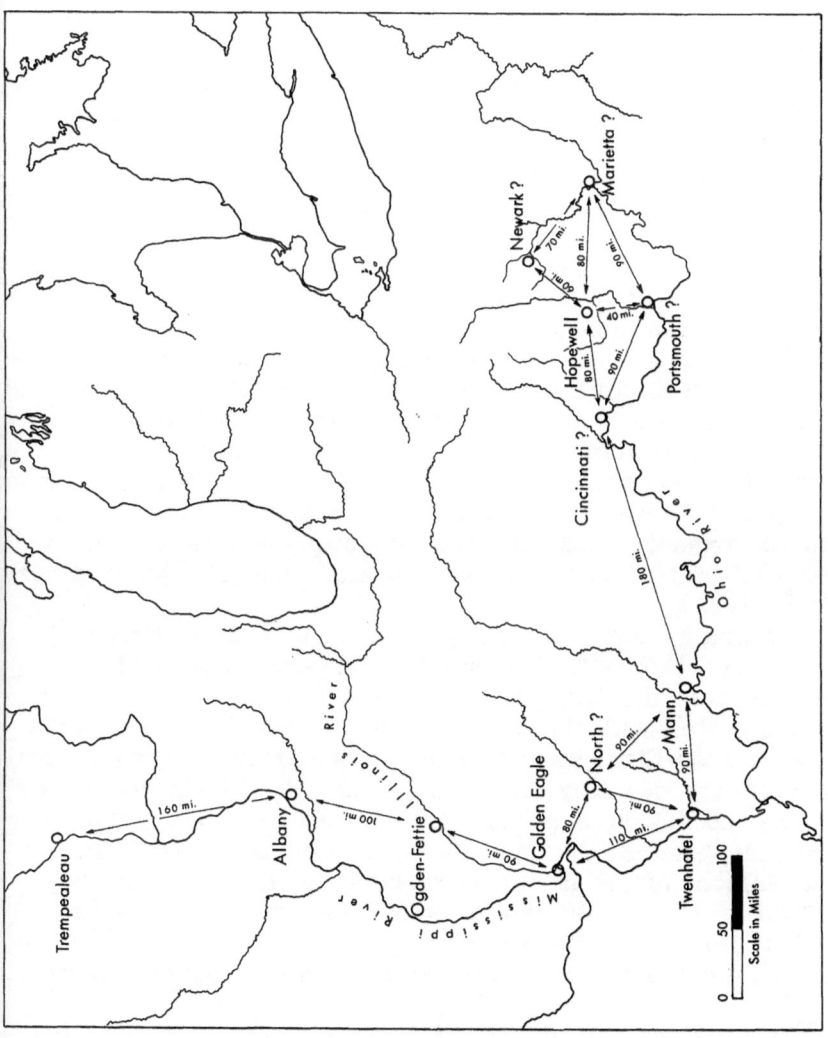

Fig. 1. Regional transaction centers of the Middle Woodland period in the Midwest-Riverine area.

Illinois Valley, lies Golden Eagle, a large geometric earthwork with associated mounds (McAdams, 1887).

The North site is situated in the central Kaskaskia Valley, eighty miles southeast of Golden Eagle. Its 6 mounds and 10 acre habitation area single it out as by far the largest known Middle Woodland site in the Kaskaskia Valley (Gregory Perino, personal communication). Ninety miles downstream from North lies the Twenhafel site whose 26 mounds and 5 habitation areas covering some 90 acres make it far larger than any known Middle Woodland site in this part of the central Mississippi Valley. The Mann site is located 90 miles due east of Twenhafel on the Ohio River in southern Indiana. James Kellar (personal communication) points out that the 7 mounds, 3 geometric earthworks and total site area of ca. 200 acres set this site apart from all other Middle Woodland sites in this section of the Ohio Valley.

Continuing east into Ohio, the literature discloses that the famous Hopewell site in south-central Ohio is unusual among the great Ohio centers for its gross size, number of mounds, special mortuary construction and quantity and diversity of Hopewell Interaction Sphere artifacts. The five other extensively excavated Middle Woodland centers in Ohio—Harness, Tremper, Mound City, Seip and Turner—range from ca. 13 to 104 acres in area and include from 2 to 22 mounds. Hopewell is larger than any of these—132 acres—and discloses 10 more mounds than the next largest center.

The enormity and complexity of constructions at Hopewell also set it apart from the other Ohio centers. Mound 25 at Hopewell is both the largest and structurally the most complex mound associated with the Hopewell Interaction Sphere in North America; it also discloses a greater concentration of Interaction Sphere artifacts than any other single mound. The pretentious log charnel houses at Hopewell also distinguish it from the other Ohio centers (Shetrone, 1926). It is perhaps noteworthy that ritual treatment of the dead differs between Hopewell and the other Ohio centers. Whereas almost two-thirds of the bodies interred at Hopewell were not cremated, 90 to 100 percent cremation is reported for all other centers except Turner (Shetrone, 1926).

The unusual complexity of the Hopewell site is perhaps best reflected, as Winters (1964) points out, in the large caches of Interaction Sphere goods and raw materials deposited there. Approximately 8,300 hornstone disks from Mound 2, ca. 150 obsidian "ceremonial spears" from Mound 25, ca. 300 pounds of obsidian knapping debris and raw material from Mound 11, and

210 copper artifacts from two burials alone in Mound 25 are but
a few examples. Also distinguishing Hopewell from the other
Ohio centers are: *a*) the many large caches of a particular imported raw material; *b*) the manufacture of an almost unique
class of artifacts from a specific mineral (e.g., the copper cutout figures, crystal quartz boatstones and cones, etc.); and *c*)
the occurrence of exotic raw materials that are rare or absent
elsewhere in Ohio (e.g., iron pyrites). All these characteristics
suggest that Hopewell functioned as a major receiving, manufacturing and transaction center in the Ohio region of the Hopewell Interaction Sphere.

Hopewell clearly stands apart from the other Ohio Middle
Woodland sites as a major manufacturing center. The masses
of raw material, preforms and manufacturing debris of a number
of exotic minerals (hornstone, obsidian and copper) support this
interpretation. In addition, many examples of each of a number
of artifact classes, all made from one imported raw material,
would suggest that Hopewell was both a receiving and a manufacturing center for that raw material. Excavations there disclose
more than 60 axes from one mound alone, also more than 125
earspools, 60 breastplates and 30 bracelets, not to mention other
less numerous artifact classes, all made of copper. Unaltered
copper nuggets were also recovered. It appears that copper was
brought into the Hopewell site and there manufactured into certain classes of artifacts, examples of which were later distributed
in the Interaction Sphere.

This apparent differentiation between Ohio centers in the
scale of ritual activity reflected in gross site size, complexity
of earthworks and mortuary constructions, and quantity and diversity of Interaction Sphere goods indicates that the simple picture
of a regional center functioning for the receipt and distribution
of trade goods is inadequate. Clearly, Mound City, Harness and
the other centers played an important role in the interaction network. However, none equals the size and complexity of Hopewell.
Furthermore, none of these sites reflects the scale of ritual-related manufacturing activity seen at Hopewell.

In size and elaborateness of earth construction, the Cincinnati, Portsmouth and Marietta sites more closely resemble Hopewell than do the other Ohio centers, with the exception of Newark.
All three were destroyed by the growth of Ohio River cities before they could be extensively investigated, though all were mapped
beforehand by Squier and Davis (1848) or Whittlesey. The 3
geometric earthworks at Marietta encompassed 95 acres and 16
mounds; at least 3 of the mounds were truncated pyramids.

Portsmouth was comprised of 3 groups of earthworks encompassing an estimated total of 100 acres and connected by 16 miles of earth embankments (Squier and Davis, 1848:Pl. 27). The destruction of the Cincinnati center was far advanced by the days of Squier and Davis. Nonetheless, fragments of information suggest it involved a complex series of geometric earthworks and mounds in what is today downtown Cincinnati (Starr, 1960).

Cincinnati, Portsmouth, and Marietta, standing at the mouths of three of the four major rivers leading North from the Ohio, were positioned to control the flow of goods into this area. These particularly large and complex sites represent, it is hypothesized, major centers maintaining close transactional ties with the structurally comparable Hopewell center, enabling them together to control movement of Interaction Sphere goods into and within the Ohio region. By the same token, the smaller Seip Mound City, and Harness sites in the Paint Creek--Scioto confluence locality might be seen as centers for local level receipt and distribution of trade goods. What is perhaps emerging from these gross structural differences in Ohio Middle Woodland sites is the picture of a hierarchy of transaction centers articulated in a complex set of goods distribution systems.

To extend this picture, we are reminded of the assertion that the Hopewell Interaction Sphere is characterized by the sharing of imported minerals and marine products among a number of regional Middle Woodland cultures. Traded as unaltered raw material, preforms or finished products were copper, mica, obsidian, marine shells, pipestone, crystal quartz, chlorite, meteoric iron and various siliceous materials from Knife River (North Dakota) chalcedony to southern Illinois and Indiana "hornstone" to Flint Ridge flint. Yet, Table 1 shows that many of these and other less important exotic materials were concentrated in only a few regions. Furthermore, it is amazing how few artifact classes (or formal styles within classes) made from the copper, mica, marine shells, bear teeth, pipestone and the other quantitatively important raw materials moving through the Interaction Sphere are actually shared by the various participating regional and local Middle Woodland cultures. Note, for example, in Figure 2 and Table 2 the differential distribution of the various artifact classes and styles made from these raw materials when comparing mortuary goods recovered from Middle Woodland sites in just two regions, Ohio and Illinois.

From the preceding evidence of both gross structural differences in Middle Woodland sites within a region and the variable distribution of Interaction Sphere goods within and between

TABLE 1

DIFFERENTIAL DISTRIBUTION OF MAJOR HOPEWELL INTERACTION SPHERE RAW MATERIALS IN THE MIDWEST-RIVERINE AREA
(By Locality)

	Ohio-Paint Creek-Scioto	Ohio-Scioto Mouth	Ohio-Little Miami	Lower Illinois Valley	Central Illinois Valley	Upper Mississippi Valley
Copper	1,422	45	914	47	156	438
Mica	3,793	112	77	6	6	—
Obsidian	10,126	—	11	11	—	2
Bear Canine Teeth	242	—	42	39	239	12
Crystal Quartz	1,350	2	—	1	—	—
Pearls	32,565	—	16,022	469	3,007	22
Silver	37	—	8	10	120	11
Galena	149	4	7	5	3	1
Meteoric Iron	34	—	35	6	22	—
Marine Products	194	—	29	24	19	—

Note–The data presented on Table 1 are as accurate an account as possible working from the site reports alone. In many cases, the report included only references such as "several bear canine teeth." Therefore, the data included in the table represent at times a minimum number of artifacts; however, the *relative* amounts of artifacts are representative of their actual distribution.

The pearl and metal artifact counts may be misleading. Pearl slug beads were variably described as either "necklaces," raw counts of the number of beads found, or else no quantitative data at all were given. As a result, the data are not strictly comparable between sites. Copper or silver beads were usually counted, thereby skewing the number of artifacts made from these raw materials. For instance, the 120 silver artifacts recorded for the central Illinois Valley represented a single necklace.

regions, it is possible to begin the task of defining both interlocal and interregional interaction networks. The outlines of these networks are recognizable in the variable distribution of Interaction Sphere products as reflected in:

   a) differences between sites, localities and regions in the kinds and quantities of exotic raw material occurring there;
   b) differences in the classes of artifacts manufactured from these exotic materials;
   c) within-class differences in styles; and
   d) differences in behavior relating to receipt, use and final deposition (or "banking") of these Interaction Sphere goods.

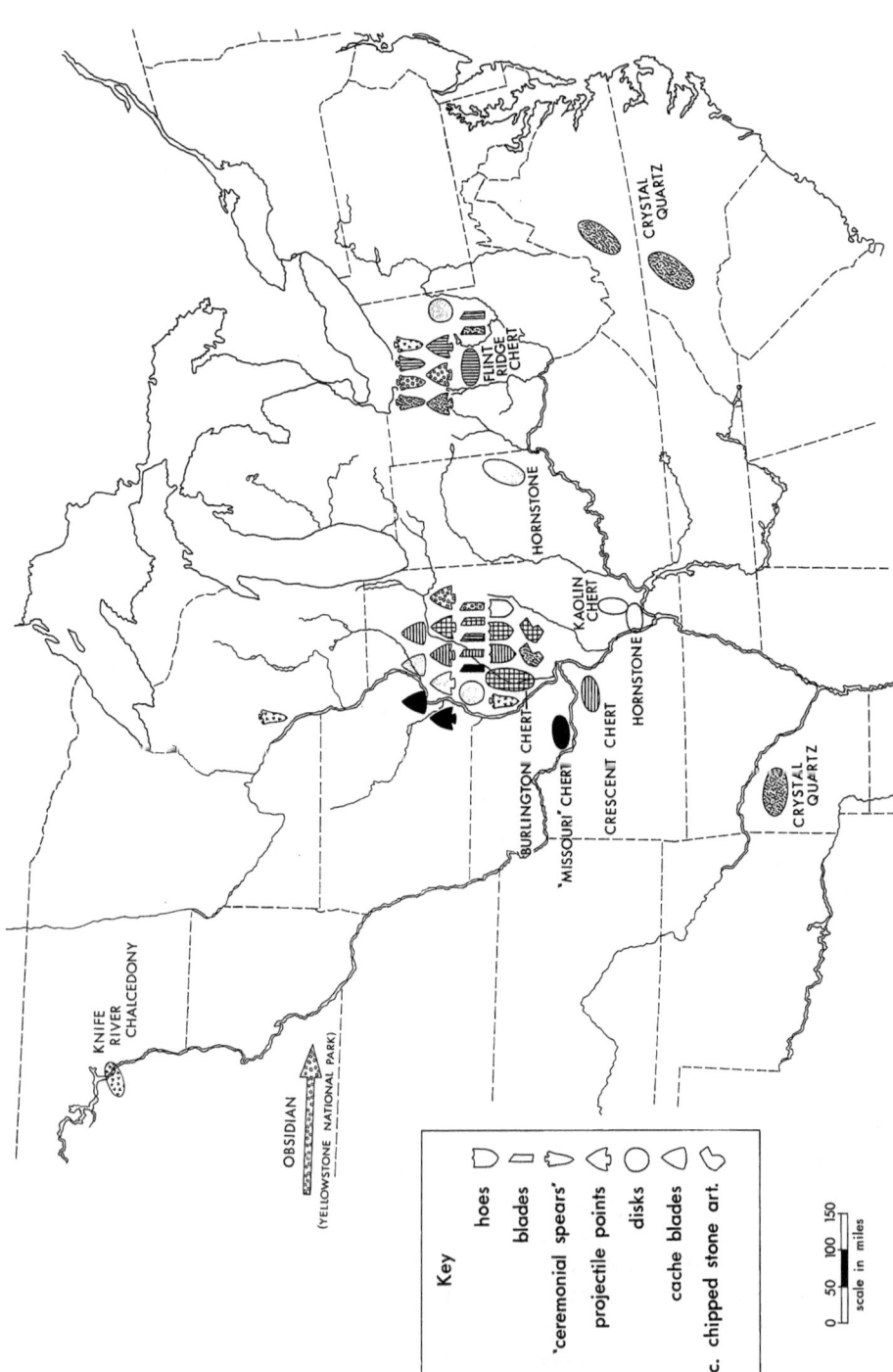

Fig. 2. Differential distribution in Ohio and Illinois of various artifact classes and imported raw materials characterizing the Hopewell Interaction Sphere.

TABLE 2
OCCURRENCE OF HOPEWELL ARTIFACT CLASSES AND STYLES IN OHIO AND ILLINOIS
(By Raw Material)

	OHIO	ILLINOIS
Obsidian	Projectile Points Lamellar Flakes Ceremonial Spears	Projectile Points Lamellar Flakes
Mica	Trimmed Sheets Cut-Out Figures	Trimmed Sheets
Copper	Awls Earspools Beads Adzes Celts Headplates Pan Pipes Rings Buttons Cut-Out Figures Cones Bracelets	Awls Earspools Beads Adzes Celts Headplates Pan Pipes Rings Buttons Cut-Out Figures
Crystal Quartz	Lamellar Flakes Ceremonial Spears Plummets Boatstones Cones	Pendant
Bear Canine Teeth	Cut Drilled Split Pearl Inlaid Pegged Carved Hinged Incised Hollowed-Out	Cut Drilled Split Pearl Inlaid

Platform Pipes	Effigy
	Plain: Smokestack
	      Monitor
	      T-Shaped
		Effigy
		Plain: Smokestack
		      Monitor
		      V-Based

References used for compiling frequency data in Tables 1 and 2:

Ohio—Paint Creek—Scioto: Hopewell (Shetrone and Greenman, 1931), Seip (Shetrone and Greenman, 1931), Mound City (Shetrone and Greenman, 1931), and Harness (Shetrone and Greenman, 1931).

Ohio—Scioto Mouth: Tremper (Shetrone and Greenman, 1931).

Ohio—Little Miami: Turner (Shetrone and Greenman, 1931).

Lower Illinois Valley: Bedford (Perino, n.d.*a*), Brangenberg (Baker, et al., 1941), Gibson (Struever, 1968; Perino, 1968), Hardin (Thomas, 1894), Kamp (Baker, et al., 1941; Struever, 1960), Klunk (Perino, 1968), Meppen (Fecht, 1955; Perino, n.d.*b*), Meredosia (Struever, 1968), Merrigan (McAdams, 1884; Struever, 1968), Montezuma (Fowke, 1905; Perino, n.d.*a*), Mound House (Struever, 1968), Naples—Chambers (Henderson, 1884), Peisker (Perino, 1966*a*,*b*), Pilot's Peak (Perino, n.d.*a*) and Swartz (Perino, n.d.*a*).

Central Illinois Valley: Baehr (Walton, Connolly, and Fowler, 1962), Clear Lake (Cole and Deuel, 1937), Havana (Baker, et al., 1941; McGregor, 1952), Liverpool (Cole and Deuel, 1937), Ogden-Fettie (Cole and Deuel, 1937), and Sister's Creek (Cole and Deuel, 1937).

Upper Mississippi Valley: Trempealeau (McKern, 1931).

The evidence presented in the following discussion shows that the Hopewell Interaction Sphere was not a single, homogeneous unit involving the sharing of a number of exotic raw materials and artifact styles by local Middle Woodland groups throughout the area from New York to Kansas, Michigan to Florida. Emerging instead is a picture of a number of interaction networks, of different types and on different scales. It remains to delineate more sharply the boundaries and formal characteristics of these networks and to determine the mechanisms of goods distribution within and between each.

THE INTERLOCAL NETWORK

The Golden Eagle site (McAdams, 1887:80), located exactly at the confluence of the Illinois and Mississippi rivers, represents the only known Middle Woodland geometric earthwork in the lower Illinois Valley, and as such is structurally different from any other contemporary site in this region. With its associated mounds, it bears the closest resemblance of any lower Illinois site to the Ohio Hopewell centers.

Golden Eagle probably represents a regional transaction center. Its function, we might predict, was to articulate lower Illinois Middle Woodland groups with each other and them, in turn, with groups outside the region. In this model, Interaction Sphere goods arriving in the lower Illinois region came to

Golden Eagle where transactions took place resulting in their dispersal among Middle Woodland groups in the surrounding region.

To illustrate the concept of a regional or *interlocal* interaction network integrated around such a transaction center, we note that six constructionally similar Middle Woodland cemetery-habitation sites occur on raised elevations in the Illinois Valley floodplain, spaced at relatively equal intervals beginning 14 miles north of the Golden Eagle site, and extending up the Illinois to a point 75 miles from the river mouth (see Fig. 3).

Merrigan, Kamp, Mound House, Naples-Chambers, Hilderbrand and Baehr are not only structurally similar, and therefore quite different as a group from Golden Eagle, but all are located in the Illinois Valley floodplain, on or close to the present river channel. Each involves a mound cemetery dominated by one or two loaf-shaped mounds. This mound form sharply distinguishes these sites from the other six known Middle Woodland mound cemeteries in the floodplain and the eleven known mound cemeteries on the bluff crests along the margins of the lower Illinois Valley. These loaf-shaped mounds are oval or elliptical in plan view and flat-topped in longitudinal cross section. They are also conspicuously larger than the conical mounds which characterize Hopewell mound cemeteries in the lower Illinois Valley region. Beginning at the Golden Eagle regional center which, it is recalled, is located at the very southern end of the Illinois Valley at the river mouth, the distances between these sites are 14, 15, 11 1/2, 16 1/2, 8 and 7 miles respectively (see Fig. 3).

It is possible that these six sites, with their formal mound similarities, their riverside floodplain location, their relatively even spacing along the valley, and accompanying habitation area in each case, all represent *local transaction centers*. It can be hypothesized that these sites were the focal points of economic-political-ritual activities which functioned to distribute among the local communities associated with each both the Interaction Sphere goods produced elsewhere within the lower Illinois Valley and those coming in from other points in one or more interregional networks.

We might, therefore, define minimally six local transaction centers within the southernmost 75 miles of the Illinois Valley, each involved in the accumulation and dispersal of Interaction Sphere goods within the local area surrounding it. In this model, goods arriving at Golden Eagle by means of the interregional interaction network were distributed within the lower Illinois Valley by means of activities associated with these six local

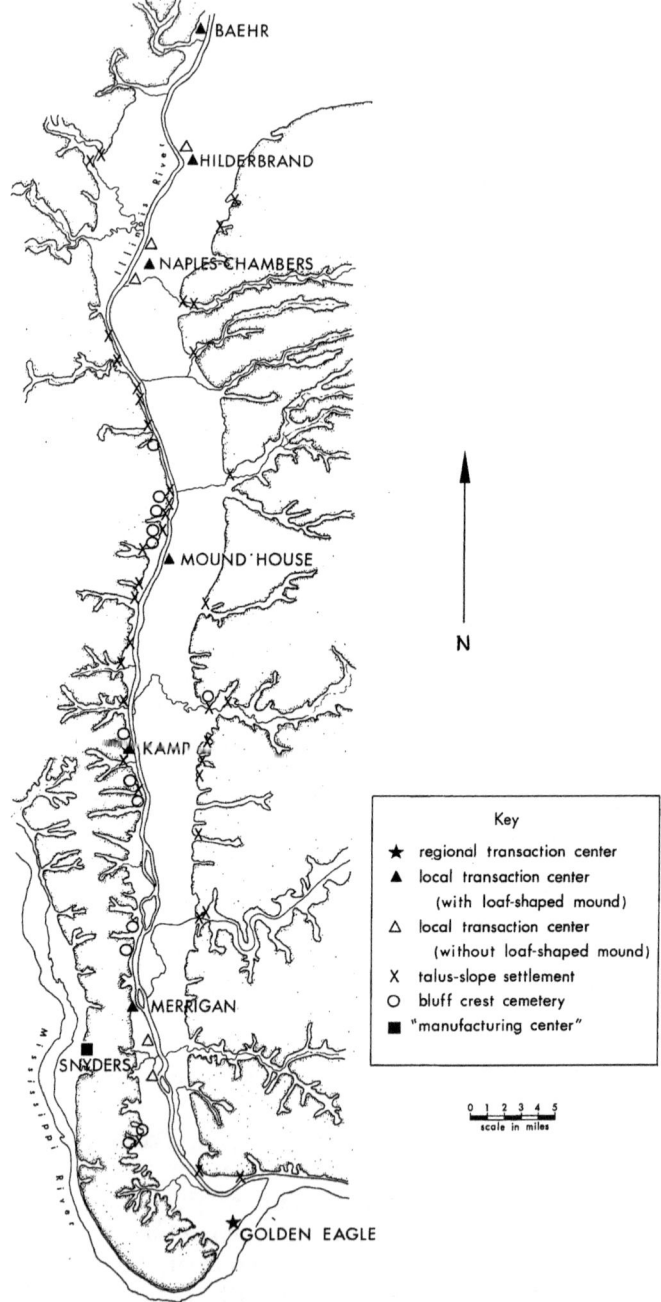

Fig. 3. Sites associated with an interlocal interaction network in the lower Illinois River Valley.

nodes. In turn, freshwater pearls or other goods destined to move into the interregional network accumulated initially at these six local centers and subsequently moved out of the lower Illinois region altogether through economic-political-ritual activities associated with the Golden Eagle regional center.

Eleven known Hopewell mound cemeteries in the lower Illinois Valley are located on the bluffcrests along the valley margins. None of these cemeteries have habitation areas adjacent to them. Instead, the Middle Woodland settlements are located on the talus slope at the base of the bluffs (cf. Fig. 3). However, all twelve Hopewell mound cemeteries located on elevated ground in the valley floodplain, including six that lack a loaf-shaped mound, have adjoining habitation areas. In fact, these twelve floodplain Middle Woodland cemetery-habitation sites share all the characteristics listed above for the local transaction center, except for the loaf-shaped mound form.

Whether we include only six or all twelve floodplain sites in our model of the local node, we might predict the recovery of high frequencies of Hopewell Interaction Sphere goods from their associated habitation areas. We might also predict that seasonality analysis would disclose that these floodplain sites were occupied during a specific time of the year in contrast to long-term, if not year-round, occupation of the settlements on the talus slopes at the valley margins. The evidence from Apple Creek supports the hypothesis that these talus slope sites were occupied all or most of the year (Struever, 1968).

In this light, it is interesting that the surface of Mound House, one of the hypothesized local transaction centers, has produced an unusual quantity and diversity of Interaction Sphere goods. In an earlier paper (Struever, 1968), we noted that the artifact and feature assemblages at the Peisker site, unlike those at Apple Creek, suggested that the occupation there was specifically oriented toward ritual activities associated with burial of the dead. An alternative hypothesis might be that the ritual activity, including burial, was all part of a seasonal pattern of ceremonial and economic functions which served to distribute Interaction Sphere goods coming into or leaving the locality.

In sum, the Mound House and Peisker data support the hypothesis that the twelve Middle Woodland floodplain cemetery-habitation sites strung along the southernmost 75 miles of the Illinois River served as local centers for the receipt and dispersal of Interaction Sphere goods in the context of ceremonial-economic-political activities which functioned to integrate their associated sociopolitical units.

It is possible to illustrate the functioning of such an interlocal network by tracing the manufacture and distribution of a single artifact style.

Located in the Mississippi Valley between the Missouri hematite sources on the one hand and the lower Illinois Valley Middle Woodland sites on the other, the Snyders site is noteworthy for the quantities of hematite plummets and apparent plummet preforms recovered there. The predominant plummet style is named Snyders Grooved (Fig. 6; Perino, 1961). A recent study by Lynne Goldstein (n.d.) indicates that Snyders Grooved plummets are spread throughout the lower Illinois Valley region, occurring on Middle Woodland habitation sites or as isolated surface finds. This plummet form appears relatively infrequently elsewhere in the Midwest Riverine area.

It might be hypothesized from these data that raw hematite or hematite plummet preforms moved into the Snyders community where they were worked into a distinctive plummet form, numbers of which were subsequently distributed through transactions at a local center, perhaps the Peisker site in this case. These transactions at Peisker involved individuals or groups associated with Merrigan, Kamp and other local centers up and down the Illinois River. Through this interlocal or regional network, Snyders Grooved plummets moved into the sociopolitical units associated with these other centers and, through a repetition of these transactions, spread to the limits of the regional network.

This transactional system is diagrammed for the lower Illinois Valley in Figure 4. Included are names of the specific bluffcrest cemeteries and talus slope settlements believed to be associated with the local transaction centers used for illustration in the diagram. In this manner, analysis of the distribution of styles of a single artifact produced at a localized, identifiable manufacturing site may allow the archaeologist to establish the limits of the transactional network involving that artifact style.

CONCENTRATING AREAS FOR INTERACTION SPHERE RAW MATERIALS

The majority of Hopewell Interaction Sphere raw materials tend to be highly visible, scarce, durable, transportable and available from localized source areas only. Four possible major source localities can be identified, each yielding multiple raw materials. These source areas are the Rocky Mountains, the Lake Superior region, the lower Allegheny Mountains and the

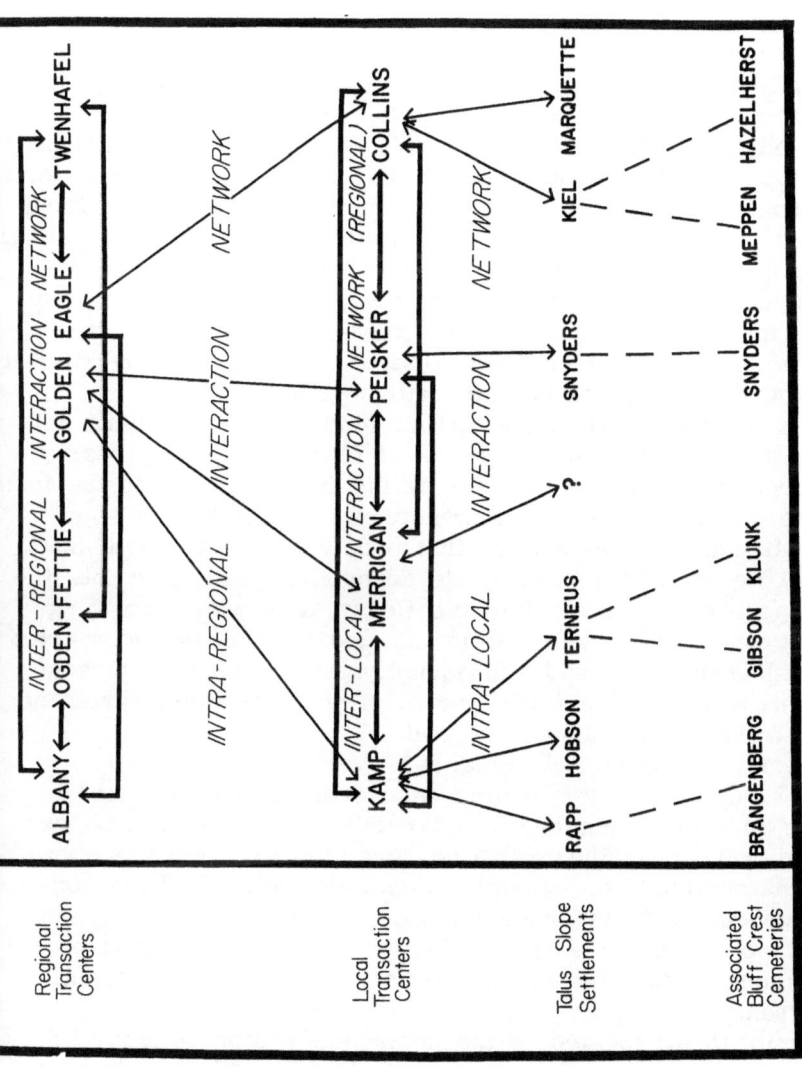

Fig. 4. A heirarchy of interaction networks illustrated by specific Illinois Middle Woodland sites believed to exemplify the various settlement types involved.

south Atlantic-Gulf Coastal region (cf. Fig. 5). All are far-distant from the recipient Middle Woodland groups located, for the most part, within the major river systems of the eastern deciduous woodlands. Other raw materials, such as hornstone chert and Ohio pipestone, occur within the area of the interacting groups.

Distribution of the raw material sources, combined with the evidence for these imports at the six Ohio Middle Woodland centers, reflects differential access to these materials among the centers.

As Figure 5 discloses, the Hopewell obsidian (Griffin, Gordus and Wright, 1969) and, quite likely, any grizzly bear canine teeth came from the Rocky Mountains. Except for drift copper from glacial tills, it is believed that Hopewell native copper and silver came from Isle Royale and/or the Keweenaw Peninsula in the Lake Superior region. In addition, Shetrone (1926:217) suggests that the micaceous hematite occurring exclusively at the Hopewell site is the "foliated, highly lustrous variety, exactly similar to that now being mined at Marquette, Michigan . . ."

It is noteworthy that, among the Ohio Middle Woodland centers, by far the greatest quantities of obsidian, grizzly bear teeth, copper and hematite occur at the Hopewell site in the form of unaltered raw material, manufacturing debris and finished goods. It can be hypothesized that people associated with the Hopewell center had special trade connections extending into the Lake Superior region and into the Rocky Mountains, providing them access to these four exotic materials which they converted into finished artifacts and subsequently traded, along with some of the unaltered raw material itself, to their contemporaries at centers in Ohio and perhaps beyond.

Whereas Hopewell was clearly a *concentrating area* for a number of exotic materials dispersed over the Great Lakes-Riverine area via a number of interaction networks, it does not appear to have been the exclusive receiving area for these imported materials. For example, Hopewell seems to have controlled receipt and dispersal of copper in the Ohio region, but does not appear to have had exclusive control of this native metal among Middle Woodland groups over the broader Great Lakes area.

Trempealeau, located in the upper Mississippi Valley, exhibits large quantities of copper (and silver) artifacts when compared with other extra-Ohio sites. This may reflect its proximity to the source area—the Lake Superior region.

That Trempealeau was in fact procuring its own copper and silver directly from the source area, and not relying on its

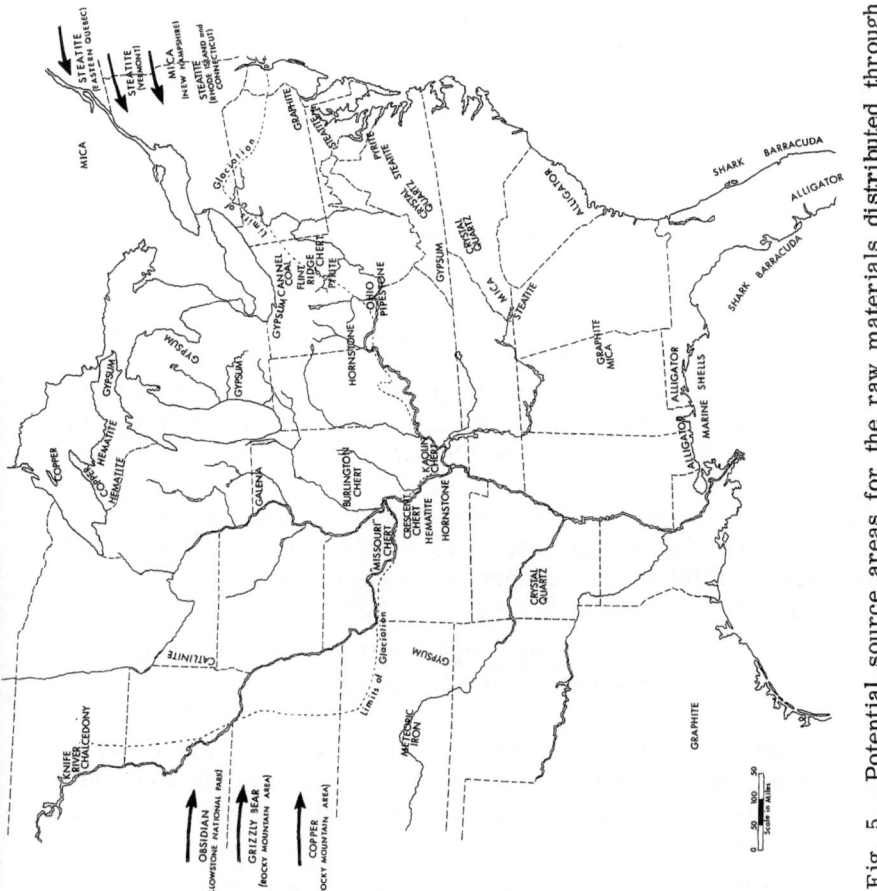

Fig. 5. Potential source areas for the raw materials distributed through the Hopewell Interaction Sphere.

dispersal from the Ohio centers, is evidenced in two ways. First, although relatively rich in copper, Trempealeau lacks many of the other Interaction Sphere goods, notably mica and marine products, which appear to have moved with copper through the interregional networks and are therefore common occurrences in other regions. If Trempealeau was in fact obtaining its copper through an interregional system involving Ohio, it might be expected to show evidence of intensive trade in these other exotic materials as well. This is not the case, suggesting that Trempealeau's access to copper did not depend upon an interregional trade system whose nucleus was central Ohio.

Second, the region which has the next largest amount of copper and silver outside the Ohio area is the central Illinois Valley, which is geographically close to the Trempealeau center. Since the lower Illinois Valley has little copper or silver compared with the central valley, it appears that this raw material was not coming into the central Illinois Valley by way of the Ohio, Mississippi and Illinois rivers, the most convenient route if it were being brought in from Ohio, but was instead moving south via transactions with the Trempealeau center in the upper Mississippi Valley.

In sum, Trempealeau appears to have functioned as a second concentrating area for at least two raw materials important in the Hopewell Interaction Sphere.

TRANSACTIONAL RELATIONSHIPS AMONG THE OHIO HOPEWELL CENTERS

Quantitative analysis of exotic raw materials and finished artifacts enable us to reconstruct the patterns of interaction between a number of Ohio Middle Woodland centers. This involves analysis of:

a) exotic raw materials with specific, designatable source locations;
b) styles of artifacts made from these raw materials;
c) unaltered raw materials, preforms and debris, all of which reflect the manufacturing process; and
d) the spatial distribution of all of these among six Ohio Middle Woodland local and regional transaction centers.

By considering the manufacturing process, by distinguishing unaltered raw material from preforms, and the latter from finished goods, and by plotting the distribution of the unaltered raw materials, manufacturing debris and various styles of finished goods among the six Ohio centers, it is possible to develop models for the transactional relationships among them.

It is possible, when assessing the distribution of Interaction Sphere goods among the six Ohio centers, to suggest local specialization in the production of Interaction Sphere artifacts. This is reflected, as Winters (1964) points out, in the frequent localization at one or two centers of artifacts made from specific raw materials. Thus, ca. 150 of the large ceremonial spears were recovered at Hopewell while only a few of these spears occurred at the other five Ohio centers. That obsidian artifact manufacture was a Hopewell specialty may be reflected in some 300 pounds of obsidian chipping debris and raw material found in Hopewell Mound 11. Moorehead (1922) describes excavating "nearly a bushel of fragments" of quartz artifacts at Hopewell; Shetrone and Greenman (1931) list 1,347 quartz artifacts from Hopewell. The remaining Ohio centers disclose in each case only one or two artifacts made from this raw material. These data, together with the occurrence of artifact classes of crystal quartz unique to the Hopewell site (e.g. boatstones and cones), suggest that this was the center for manufacturing artifacts of this raw material. More than 3,000 mica artifacts, including the largest number of mica geometric and representational figures occurring in any Ohio center, were recovered at Hopewell, together with sizeable quantities of mica raw material and manufacturing debris.

Mica was also important at Mound City where several large caches of that raw material occurred. Mound City also appears to have been the center of galena distribution since 100 galena items were recorded; this is more than three times the number of galena items found in any of the other five sites.

The Tremper site yielded far and away the greatest number of plain platform pipes, the majority of which are represented by two distinct styles—the T-shaped and Smokestack varieties (Fig. 6). On the other hand, Shetrone and Greenman (1931) calculated that over 200 effigy platform pipes, largely of Ohio pipestone, were recovered at Mound City, a figure more than three times that of any of the other Ohio centers.

The high degree of homogeneity at Tremper of both the T-shaped and Smokestack pipes is suggestive of a local industry. It can be hypothesized that, with their control of the Ohio pipestone sources near Portsmouth, Middle Woodland groups associated with Tremper manufactured a very consistent plain platform pipe style, referred to here as the Smokestack variety,

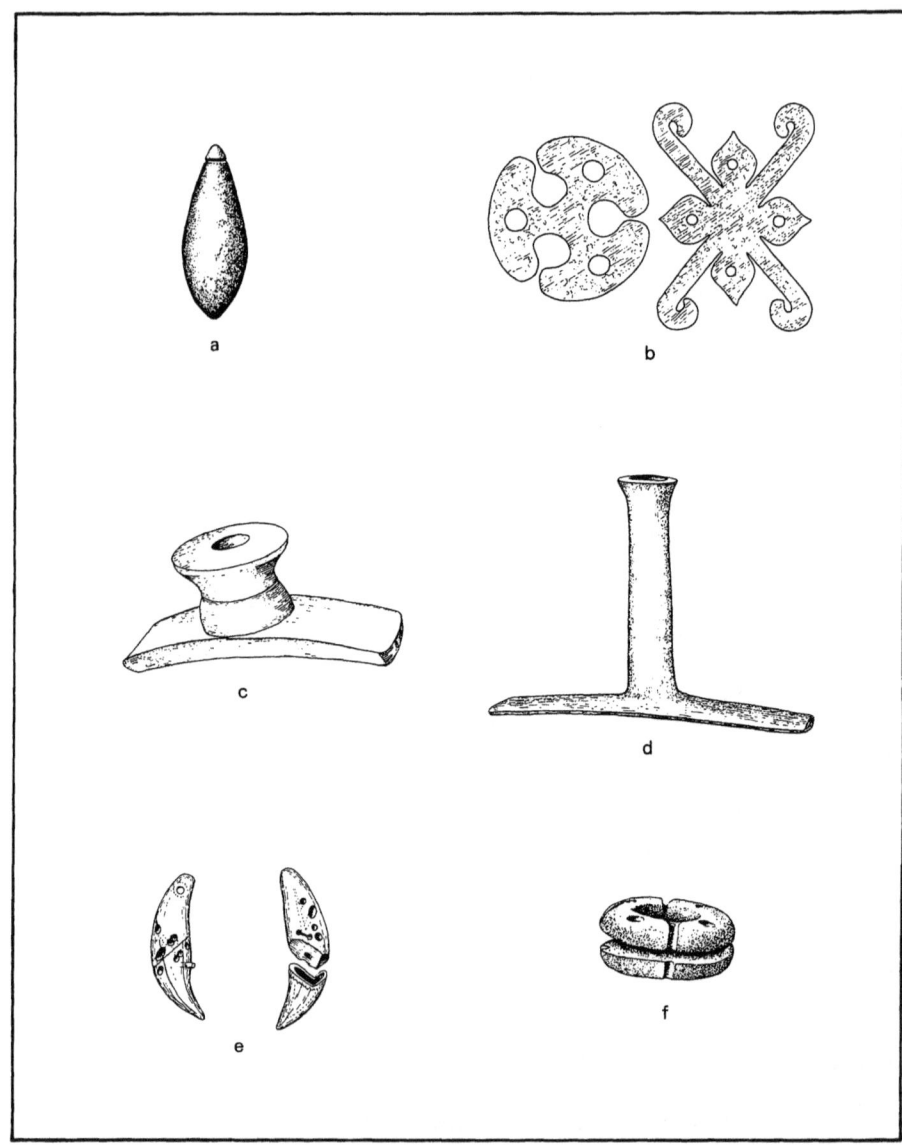

Fig. 6. Hopewell Interaction Sphere artifacts: *a* Snyders Grooved plummet; *b* Copper cut-out figures; *c* Smokestack platform pipe; *d* T-shaped platform pipe; *e* Split, drilled and pegged bear canine teeth; *f* Copper earspool, hamburger bun style.

which they traded to the other Ohio centers, particularly Mound City. It is noteworthy that, next to Tremper, Mound City yields the largest number of plain platform pipes (15) of any Ohio center, and many of these are in the Tremper Smokestack style. The relatively small number of effigy platform pipes at Tremper compared with their great frequency at Mound City suggests that the Tremper inhabitants traded pipestone raw material to Mound City where local artisans carved effigy pipes, some of which were traded back to Tremper for Smokestack pipes and pipestone raw material. This hypothesis of reciprocal transactions between Mound City and Tremper is corroborated by the occurrence of a distinctive reel-shaped gorget style which in Ohio occurs exclusively at these two sites.

The hypothesis for two local pipe industries can be tested by a detailed analysis of the Mound City and Tremper effigy pipe styles to ascertain the degree of within- and between-site similarity. If the Tremper effigy pipes were made exclusively at Mound City, they should reflect the same range of style variation seen in the Mound City effigy pipes themselves.

A similar comparative analysis could be undertaken with the Tremper and Mound City Smokestack pipes to determine whether they represent one or more styles. That plain platform pipes were manufactured at Tremper would seem to be demonstrated by the exclusive occurrence of the T-shaped style at that site.

Other indications of the economic relationships between the Ohio Middle Woodland centers suggest themselves. Mound City (Mills, 1922) discloses a number of large caches of sheet mica which might be regarded as preforms for the manufacture of geometric and representational figures which occur in by far the greatest numbers at the Hopewell site. We might hypothesize that the Mound City inhabitants specialized in the separation of the mica books into thin sheets or plates, the edges of which were cut and abraded preparatory to shipment to Hopewell, where artisans manufactured the various cutout forms which were subsequently traded to the other Ohio centers. In exchange for the Mound City mica, the Hopewell inhabitants may have shipped copper cutouts which, from the large number occurring at Hopewell, appear to represent a local production. It is noteworthy, in lieu of good quantitative data, that Shetrone (1926) indicates that Mound City was the only other Ohio center in which copper cutouts were "abundant."

That Hopewell was a manufacturing center for copper items in Ohio is corroborated by the exclusive occurrence at that site of the "Hamburger bun" style of earspool (Fig. 6). This appears to be a local copper earspool style made in small quantities and not traded.

It appears that the inhabitants at Hopewell had exclusive access to the obsidian raw material sources, as reflected in the over 10,000 obsidian items documented there, in contrast to 50 or less items at the other five centers. Mound City not only yields the second greatest amount of obsidian, but it is the only center besides Hopewell in which quantities of obsidian ceremonial spears occur. It appears that these spears were moving from Hopewell to Mound City, perhaps in exchange for the trimme mica sheets.

Manufacture of bear canine ornaments was centered at the Hopewell site. This can be argued both on the basis of the differentially high frequencies of bear tooth ornaments uncovered there ("several hundreds" by Moorehead (1922) alone) and by the exclusive appearance here of the elaborately cut, drilled, pegged, inlaid, mended, hinged, split, incised and hollowed-out teeth which do not appear elsewhere in Ohio or beyond (Fig. 6). If, as argued, Hopewell was the chief, if not exclusive, recipient in the Ohio region of grizzly bear canines from the Rocky Mountain area, it appears that a portion of the canine imports were used on the elaborate bear tooth ornaments which were made and held locally, while the remaining canines were traded to the other Ohio centers and beyond, either unworked or as simply drilled and/or split artifacts.

In sum, the artifacts characteristic of the Ohio regional interaction network would include the large, pulley-type stone rings (Fig. 7); the miniature sculptures-in-the-round-decorated human long bones (Fig. 7); and the geometric and representational copper and mica cutout figures.

Trade among the Ohio Middle Woodland centers also apparently involved the unaltered exotic raw materials, since several of the centers reveal artifact styles not seen at the other centers. At Hopewell, for example, the hamburger bun copper earspools, copper finger rings, elaborately carved bear canines, and ground crystal quartz geometric forms all appear to represent local artifact styles—and therefore local manufactures—that are nonexistent at the other Ohio centers. Another example would be the T-shaped pipe form which appears to occur exclusively at Tremper.

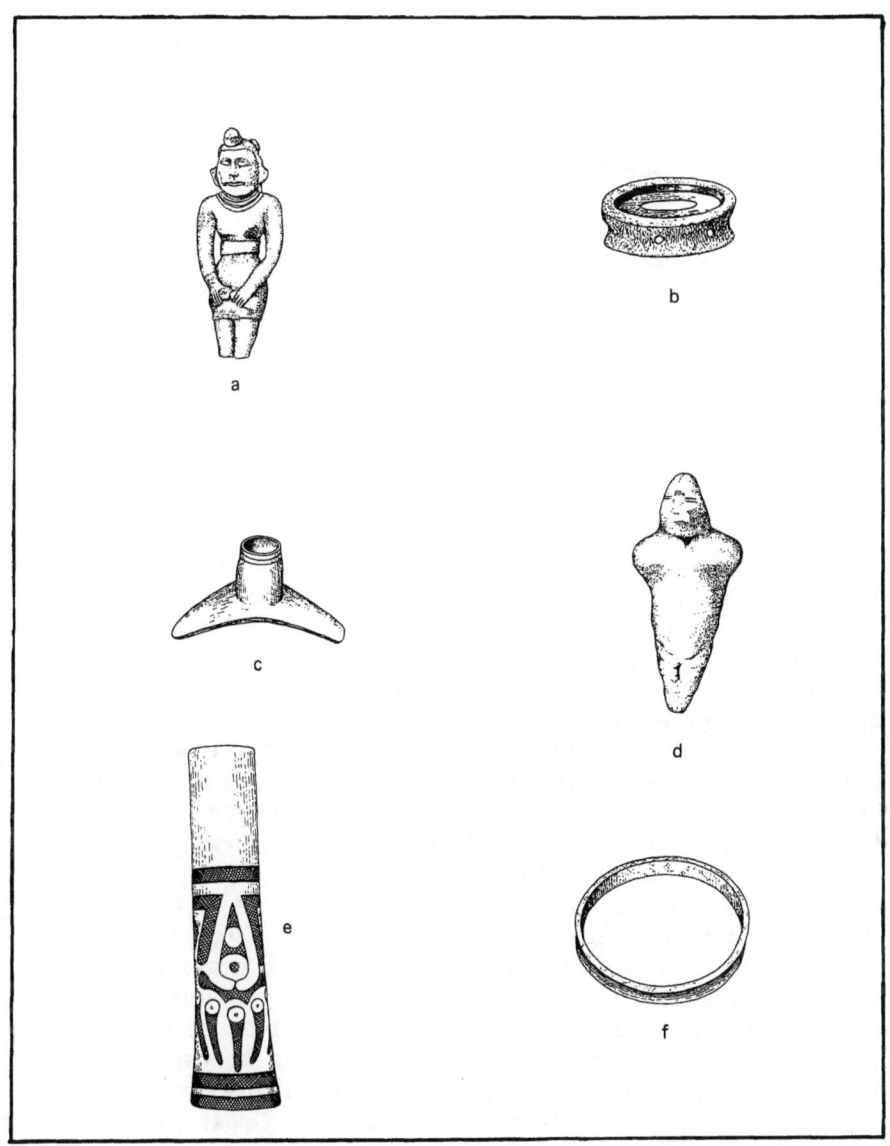

Fig. 7. Hopewell Interaction Sphere artifacts: *a* Classic Hopewell pottery figurine; *b* Pulley-type pottery earspool; *c* V-base platform pipe; *d* Pottery figurine, Casper-the-Ghost style; *e* Engraved human legbone; *f* Large stone ring.

INTERREGIONAL INTERACTION NETWORKS

It can be argued that the seven to twelve major Middle Woodland sites or site complexes discussed earlier in this paper, from Trempealeau on the north to Twenhafel on the south and Newark or Portsmouth on the east, functioned as regional transaction centers. They were not only the loci of transactions serving to integrate small-scale sociopolitical units in an interlocal interaction network, but were also nodes controlling interregional transactions which acted to regulate and reinforce ties between regional Middle Woodland elites over the larger Great Lakes area.

The wide distribution, in the Illinois Valley on the one hand, and in the Ohio Middle Woodland centers on the other, of specific artifact styles made of exotic raw material reflects this interregional network.

We might postulate that the Ohio centers shipped effigy and plain (particularly Smokestack variety) platform pipes, raw pipestone, simple bicymbal copper earspools, copper axes, trimmed mica sheets, occasional grizzly bear canines, Flint Ridge blades, and raw obsidian to Illinois Valley Middle Woodland groups in exchange for "classic" Hopewell figurines, Hopewell ware pottery, edge-drilled, pulley-type earspools of pottery, and pearls.

Meyers' (n.d.) recent study of lower Illinois Valley chert sources documents the great abundance of excellent Burlington chert there, making it quite possible that this raw material was also moved into Ohio. The gray hornstone of southern Illinois and Indiana also appears to have been imported into Ohio.

The argument for the movement into Illinois of the specific Ohio artifact styles and exotic raw materials listed above is based on the previous discussion in which, for example, the great abundance of finished obsidian artifacts, unaltered raw material and chipping debris at Hopewell enables us to argue that groups here had special (if not exclusive) access to the western obsidian sources. We have argued above that a number of imported raw materials were entering the Great Lakes-Riverine area, and the Middle Woodland interaction networks there, via the large Ohio centers—particularly Hopewell, Mound City, and others concentrated in the Paint Creek—central Scioto River area. Here they were sometimes converted into finished goods, a portion of which were traded within and beyond the Ohio region.

It is believed that the classic Hopewell figurines, Hopewell ware pottery and edge-drilled, pulley-type pottery earspools were

Illinois manufactures because they appear in relatively large numbers and in numerous sites in that region, in contrast to their scarcity in Ohio. A further argument, in the case of the Hopewell ceremonial pottery, is the fact that it shares style elements with Havana ware, the local Illinois Valley ceramic antecedent.

An alternative interpretation of the artifact styles shared by Middle Woodland groups in the Ohio and Illinois regions might be that primarily raw materials and stylistic concepts—not finished goods—were moving between the two regions. This alternative hypothesis could be tested, again, by analyzing the stylistic variability in copper axes, earspools, conjoined tubes and the other artifact classes within and between the Ohio and Illinois regions.

Pearls represent an interesting problem. To understand the reasoning behind the ascription of a primarily Illinois source to this item, it will be useful to discuss the role of the Turner site, both in the Ohio regional interaction system and in the Ohio-Illinois interregional system.

Next to Hopewell, the site with the greatest quantity and diversity of Interaction Sphere goods is Turner. Turner's strategic position in the Ohio Valley corridor between the four large Paint Creek-central Scioto centers and the entire Illinois Middle Woodland development to the west may be in part responsible for its elaboration.

It is noteworthy that Turner, along with Hopewell, yielded by far the greatest quantities of pearls and pearl artifacts among the Ohio centers, e.g., 48,000 pearls in a single "altar" (Willoughby and Hooton, 1922). We might postulate that, among the Ohio centers, Turner had closest access to the very rich pearl-producing areas of the central and lower Illinois and Wabash valleys. Among the striking characteristics of Illinois and adjacent Mississippi Valley Middle Woodland sites in western Illinois are the relatively large quantities of pearls occurring in mortuary context in association with diagnostic Hopewell Interaction Sphere artifacts. The major rivers of western (and southeastern) Illinois were, even into historic times, well-known for their large, pearl-producing mussel beds.

Pearls, then, may have been a major resource moving from Illinois to Ohio in that interregional network, with Turner occupying a pivotal position in these transactions. In return, copper bicymbal earspools and panpipes, mica sheets, obsidian, platform pipes and other goods moved west.

Within the Ohio regional network, Turner's pearls were exchanged for manufactures in copper, mica, grizzly bear teeth and obsidian, largely emanating from Hopewell whether directly or via Mound City and Seip, and for platform pipes carved by groups associated with Tremper and Mound City.

The outlines of still other Middle Woodland interregional networks present themselves. One such network is centered in the central and lower Illinois Valley and in the Mississippi Valley immediately south. This network is defined by the distribution of V-based plain platform pipes,[2] obsidian lamellar flakes ("blades" in Old World terminology) and "Casper-the-Ghost" figurines (Fig. 7), all of which represent Interaction Sphere goods that occur in some abundance in these regions, and in much lower frequencies outside of it.

Still another interregional network emerges from the distribution of specific Middle Woodland pottery styles. The high frequencies of ceramic containers, particularly Hopewell ware, in Illinois Valley Middle Woodland cemeteries suggest that this was the center for both the manufacture and trade of vessels with a special social-ceremonial function. Whereas 50 pottery vessels in Middle Woodland burial association are reported from Illinois and nearby Mississippi Valley mound cemeteries, only 9 are reported for all of the Ohio Middle Woodland centers combined (Del Monte, n.d.).

Neither finished pottery vessels nor ceramic motifs appear to have been important elements in the Ohio-Illinois interaction network; not only do the Ohio sites yield few vessels, but these lack some of the most prominent decorative attributes of the vessels found in Middle Woodland mortuary association in Illinois. For example, 12 vessels from Illinois cemeteries have a zoned straight dentate body decoration that is entirely absent in Ohio. The shallow bowl form is common in Hopewell ware in Illinois, but is absent in Ohio.

The small, finely-made Hopewell ware jars and bowls represent by far the most common mortuary ceramic in the Illinois, central Mississippi and Wabash valleys, thus appearing to define an interregional interaction network centered in these valleys with extensions up the Mississippi River into Wisconsin and into the St. Joseph, Grand and Muskegon valleys of western Michigan. It appears that the concept of small, well-made pottery vessels, used specifically as ritual paraphernalia, was moving through a

---

[2]The "V-based" variety (Fig. 7) occurs at Dickison, Ogden-Fettie, Frederick, Peisker, Snyders, and Kraske sites, all located in the Kaskaskia, Illinois and Mississippi Valleys in central and western Illinois.

western interregional network in the form of both locally rendered concepts (raptorial bird motif, crosshatched rim band, quadrilobate vessel form, etc.) and finished vessels. Thus, jars from Middle Woodland cemeteries in the Grand River Valley of western Michigan appear stylistically and technically identical to vessels from the upper and occasionally lower Illinois valleys, suggesting actual movement of the finished containers. These two regions also share the concept of the zoned straight dentate body decoration, a concept which may have moved between them with or without the containers themselves.

Still another interregional network may be reflected in the distribution of pottery figurine styles. Nancy Engle (letter to Struever, November 14, 1969), in her recent analysis of Hopewell pottery figurines, argues that the Mann site on the Ohio River in southern Indiana was a major manufacturing center for "classic" Hopewell figurines. More than 150 figurines are known from Mann, more than 10 times the number found at any other Middle Woodland site in the Great Lakes-Riverine area except for the Twenhafel site in the central Mississippi Valley. Miss Engle notes that some of the figurine fragments from Mann indicate that the artifact was broken during the firing process.

The classic style figurine, so prominent at Mann and probably manufactured there, was apparently distributed eastward into Ohio where it occurs at Turner and possibly Marietta, as well as westward into Illinois where it occurs at Twenhafel and various other sites, particularly in the Illinois Valley.

CONCLUSIONS

Caldwell (1964) has observed structural similarities in a number of historically-independent cases of interaction between regional cultures observable in the archaeological record. Among these, he mentions Hopewell, Olmec, Chavin and the Battle Axe cultures of Europe. All share a number of formal attributes. Contact between contemporary regional cultures involved movement of small quantities of scarce raw materials including minerals, native or smelted metals, marine products, etc. These appear archaeologically most often in burial association as prestige goods. These artifacts appear to have functioned in the social system largely as symbols of status. The participant societies appear in all cases to be characterized by sedentary communities (villages or towns) with supracommunity political integration reflected in special ceremonial settlements or ritual precincts in the larger communities. Movement of interaction sphere artifacts and raw materials among local and regional units is recognizable on at least three levels: a) among villages within a region; b) among nearby regional cultures; and c) among cultures scattered over a broad geographic area.

Caldwell (1964) proposes that we attempt a typology of interaction spheres. The aim might be to define one or more structural types of interaction within the range of uncivilized cultures and, further, to identify the cultural and/or physical environmental conditions prerequisite to development of a particular structural type.

However, the initial problem—one to which the present paper addresses itself—is that of defining interaction spheres on different scales and of different types.

Our discussion in this paper began by noting that the concept of a unitary Hopewell Culture appears to be both the result of archaeological sampling error, stemming from the proclivity of investigators for excavating Middle Woodland mortuary sites, and the result of attempting to define prehistoric cultures in terms of an undifferentiated trait list. We suggest, instead, that Middle Woodland culture in the eastern United States is best understood in terms of two complementary concepts—the regional tradition and the interaction sphere.

A Middle Woodland regional tradition, whose definition is based on style distributions within a series of subsistence-related artifacts, can be differentiated from a contemporary Hopewell Interaction Sphere whose definition is based on the distribution of status-related artifacts. It is noted that the distribution of tradition-defining and interaction sphere-defining artifacts are not coextensive in eastern North America. This is explained by arguing that the subsistence artifacts reflect the outlines of various, and likely differing, Middle Woodland cultural-ecological adaptations, whereas the status-related artifacts reflect interaction mechanisms that serve to maintain ties between these regional cultures, as well as between local groups within them.

Evidence is presented here to show that the Hopewell Interaction Sphere, as the latter phenomenon is called, was not a single, homogeneous unit involving the sharing of exotic raw materials by local Middle Woodland groups throughout the eastern Woodlands. We note, instead, how few diagnostic Hopewell artifact classes are shared among the various regional expressions of the interaction sphere, and how restricted and variable are the distributions of specific styles within these artifact classes.

Furthermore, a simple comparison of the contents and structure of excavated Hopewell sites in Ohio, Illinois and elsewhere indicates marked variation both within and between regions in the complexity of individual sites. It is argued here that differences between sites in gross size, complexity of earthwork and mortuary construction, and quantity and diversity of interaction sphere goods indicate that the simple picture of regional centers receiving and distributing trade goods is not adequate. Rather, these data reflect differing functions of settlements in a series of transactional systems, from small- to large-scale, through which quantities of scarce raw materials and finished goods moved.

An attempt is made here, through assessment of gross structural differences between Middle Woodland sites within a region and the variable distribution of interaction sphere goods within and between regions, to identify sites of former nodes in local, regional and interregional interaction systems. Emerging is a picture of a number of networks of different types and certainly on different scales. This paper represents no more than a preliminary attempt to approximate the boundaries and define the formal characteristics of some of these networks.

Our present efforts deal entirely with the problem of describing the structure and content of the southern Great Lakes manifestation of the Hopewell Interaction Sphere; the imposing problem before us is to explain the development of these interaction networks, their distribution, and the similarities and differences in the form and scale of interaction observable among the various regions.

ITINERANT MARKETING: AN ALTERNATIVE STRATEGY

Peter Benedict

THE study of exchange systems has come to occupy a major portion of the literature in economic anthropology. The study of marketing in both "tribal" and "peasant" economies has provided a considerable amount of useful data, albeit with what at times seems to be an inordinate emphasis upon a single factor of economic systems—the distributive. Although somewhat less emphasized than data, analytical progress can be detected in the body of this literature.

Within this expanding literature, increasing care is being taken to separate analytically various types of markets and to distinguish between markets as places and market processes which reach beyond specific arenas of exchange (Bohannan and Dalton, 1965:2). A growing tendency to obtain conceptual notions of *market* and *marketing* for use as heuristic devices has drawn upon relevant economic literature (see Belshaw, 1965:6ff; Nash, 1966:29-30). Perhaps the most striking consequence of the interest of anthropologists and economists is seen in the discussions of the growing importance which marketing assumes in the course of economic development.

A parallel development, and the concern of this paper, occurs in the debates concerning intensification of market activities and their relationship to the well-being of the economy as a whole. Taking to task the functional character of market activities in underdeveloped economies, the discussions suggest that the intensification of tertiary economic activites (which include forms of commerce and services) are not, in many economies, symptomatic of economic progress and vigor, but instead mask serious underlying economic problems. A sizable body of literature on market middlemen, the nature of market institutions, and the relation of regional market activity to the national economy bears upon this observation.

In the anthropologists' analysis of rural periodic marketing, for example, the issue of strategy and choice-making by marketeers is treated within a larger societal framework which allows statements to be generated about the nexuses existing between economy and society. From this it is asserted that the Catholic middleman in a Guatemala peasant market, his Muslim counterpart in a highland market place in Turkey, and the pious Islamic trader in Indonesia are indeed separated from one another by dissimilar economic environments and, as important, by social and cultural environments which provide different frameworks for the strategy necessary for engaging in marketing. It is suggested that the multiplicity of individuals involved in marketing in these types of economies on a full or part-time basis is not iniquitous, not economically imperfect, but rather is highly beneficial, providing vital links in a necessary chain of events. In brief, this form of intense tertiary activity in many tribal and peasant economies is *adaptive* to a given market ecology of underdevelopment and not reflective of economic progress.

Kaplan, an anthropologist, in a study of Mexican markets suggests in similar wording that:

It has somehow been argued that such markets are adaptive in "underdeveloped" economies since they perform the vital function of distributing goods by making great use of a plentiful resource, labor, and a minimal use of a scarce resource, capital. But they are only adaptive in an economy of low productivity, low purchasing power and restricted economic alternatives; in short, in an economy of "shared poverty" (Kaplan, 1965:92).

In economics, an interesting debate is similarly critical of the deceptive nature of heightened tertiary activity. In part, the discussion is stimulated by an influential thesis proposed by Colin Clark and A. G. B. Fisher in the 1940's. This argument, termed the Clark-Fisher thesis,[1] derives from observations of western industrial economies and suggests that as an economy develops, there is a corresponding shift to manufacturing first, then to tertiary activities. In the conventional classification of economic activities, tertiary production involves services ranging from distribution and commerce to domestic services and public administration. Thus, an increase in the numbers of those in commerce and services (here including those in any form of marketing) would be a consequence of, and pointer toward, an increase in the standard of living and an "inescapable reflection of economic progress" (Fisher, 1945:7).

Subsequent critics of this view have challenged the argument by offering substantive data from nonwestern economies. For

---

[1] A summary of the Clark-Fisher thesis can be found in Preston (1968:9-23). See also Colin Clark (1951) and Fisher (1945).

example, in a seminal article published in 1951 concerning an analysis of exchange systems in West Africa, the economists Bauer and Yamey suggest that in the area studied by them the large numbers of market middlemen engaged in market activity cannot be related to the well-being of the economy or "progress." Instead, they are a reflection of an economy fraught with problems of scarce capital, widely dispersed loci of low volume production, poor transport and communication networks, and a large surplus of idle larbor, displaced from agriculture, which is easily substituted for scarce capital (Bauer and Yamey, 1951).

The views of Kaplan and of Bauer and Yamey suggest that the apparently robust and healthy nature of the scope of market activities in many economies is largely a response to conditions of widespread poverty rather than an epiphenomenon of progress. Bauer and Yamey see these exchange systems as a necessary step in the transition from subsistence to exchange experienced by most economies. Somehow, these exchange systems function as receptacles filling up with or vehicles propelling along (depending on the choice of metaphor) large amounts of unskilled labor displaced from agriculture in the inevitable "phase one" of movement toward an exchange economy.

Bauer and Yamey suggest that:

... in emerging economies, the indispensable task of commodity distribution is expensive relative to available resources, capital is scarce and unskilled labor is abundant; the multiplicity of traders is the result of the mass use of unskilled labor instead of capital in the performance of the tasks of distribution (Bauer and Yamey, 1951:746-47).

These market systems, therefore, appear to be a response to an involuntary shift of labor from, in this case, agriculture to services. Market systems also seem to be adaptive, as Kaplan suggests, to a spatial and temporal economic structure of shared poverty. In also portraying marketeers as somewhat mindless pawns reacting to an ecology of low productivity and purchasing power, Shephard, in a study of Caribbean internal markets, suggests that "We must not lose sight of the fact that middlemen come into existence in response to a demand by producers and consumers for the essential services they perform" (quoted in Mintz, 1956:22).

The view that market systems and marketeers are somehow adaptive to an existing set of economic circumstances leads some to prognosticate that when the conditions accounting for certain markets disappear, so, too, will the markets and the employment available in them (Kaplan, 1965:92). Further, the implication is present that such markets, as adaptive mechanisms, occur in a particular phase of an economy's development when and where the transition from subsistence to market economy propels rural producers into distributive activities (Preston, 1968:10).

These observations and their underlying assumptions have gone a long way toward explicating some of the problems of underdeveloped economies. Peasant market systems, particularly in the form of periodic or itinerant retail marketing, are widespread in occurrence. In many cases, periodic market systems persist in economies which have long passed their supposed economic "take-off." However, the rationale behind the periodicity of internal trade in contemporary Germany (Barnum, 1966), France (Conduché, 1960:299-314), Morocco (Mikesell, 1958:494-511), Java (Dewey, 1962), and Korea (Stine, 1962), to mention but a few disparate examples, cannot be explained simply by reference to economic phase theories or by a rural economic malaise common to all countries.

Itinerant retailing is a viable livelihood for many in economies which are not usually labeled "underdeveloped." By varying their strategy of profit-taking, pursuing an expansive policy, experimenting and speculating with potential as well as real market relationships, and weighing social costs against material gain, these retailers do more than just react to economic conditions. Many, urban-based, are aggressive agents of syncretization seeking to manipulate market environments to bring about transactions. Factors underlying an urban rather than a rural economic malaise are often the prime causes of heightened itinerant retailing activities. In a number of economies where towns of a particular population size have been adversely affected by both economic developments at the national level and rising rural affluence, itinerant marketing can provide a needed alternative to a narrowing base of urban economic activities. To many for whom distributive activities are ancillary to other economic concerns, marketing and cartage activities provide important supplements to an inadequate urban-based livelihood.

Turkey provides a valuable context in which to view the several rationales for intense activity in itinerant trade. Often considered as an economy which has entered a period of sustained growth, Turkey differs significantly in many respects from countries entering a phase of transition, broadly speaking, from a subsistence to a market economy. A major segment of those individuals involved in itinerant retailing in Turkey do not originate in a rural agricultural sector adversely affected by factors of modernization such as mechanization and the shift to intensified cash cropping; a surprisingly large proportion originate in intermediate towns which have lost their importance as key regional urban and economic centers. The process emphasized in this discussion is not the massive shift from primary to tertiary economic activities, but rather is a shift from fixed urban-based tertiary functions to itinerancy in order to obtain new consumer areas. The example selected for discussion is illustrative of a form of periodic marketing of goods and services which is not adaptive to a general underdeveloped economic structure. Instead, it is a response to the historical victimization of a specific economic structure—the intermediate regional market town—within a generally progressive economy.

One of the social and economic problems facing Turkey today is a large and widespread amount of underemployed migrant labor. Most of the major urban centers are experiencing an influx of migrants who have temporarily or permanently left villages and small towns throughout Turkey to reside in and about the cities for employment purposes. Such migrants seek employment in a poorly developed labor market characterized by tertiary activities such as personal services, public administration, small-scale essentially itinerant retailing, and unskilled construction labor, which provides at best temporary employment for large numbers. As an aside, it might be noted that current population estimates for Turkey's cities have reduced validity insofar as they do not calculate the thousands who, as a part of a migrant labor force, move in and out of itinerant retailing, construction labor, and the lower ranks of bureaucracy.

Somewhat less known than the conditions in the cities are the local responses to underemployment which take place in small market towns in many regions throughout Turkey. In these once-important regional market towns, a dwindling base of local economic alternatives compels many townsmen to become more dependent upon forms of livelihood and sources of income located not only outside the town but outside the town's traditional network of interrelations. Within this process, the fortune of a number of townsmen is increasingly linked to opportunities provided by regional marketing.

A number of market towns, but by no means the majority, have witnessed such general processes of change. Historically, regional autonomy and economic isolation were pronounced factors in Turkey's national development. However, as with the notion of the self-sufficient village, a completely self-sufficient region, possessing only an internal distribution system, is a myth for Turkey. Regions were more or less functional regions, parts or settlements within a region being interconnected by certain exchanges, not all of which were economic; and most important, they were oriented toward a central place or settlement: the market town. As such, regions maintained a field of association within which a market town possessed a degree of centrality based upon the functions it provided and the quality and intensity of interconnections established with a fixed rural hinterland.

Through its leadership in religious, political, and economic concerns, the market town served as a center for mediating and coordinating regional needs. In this respect, a town's degree of regional importance was historically a precarious existence, based as it was upon the functions it performed. Two relationships obtained. The character of a town's activities was highly dependent upon the character of a town's sphere of influence. Conversely, through its mediating functions, a town extended an impress upon its region. The town's attraction for this hinterland was, at best, a discontinuous one based upon a region's periodic need for town services. As a result of a complicated process of historical changes, a number of market towns have experienced a decided loss of their traditional sphere of influence. The functional integration of regions has markedly altered in two basic ways, producing a new field of association in which the market town, the node, is no longer significant. First, functions which were once exclusively urban-based in the market town have shifted, as a result of structural changes at the village level, to the village, giving individual villages new regional importance. Second, other functions, also once exclusively assigned to market towns, have been transferred upward in settlement hierarchy to large urban settlements as a part of regional reorganization. In short, new regions, or fields of association, have been formed in which the market town, divested in large part of its role as mediating and coordinating center, has been forced to redefine its activities.

The loss of a town's centrality through a decline in its functions poses a severe problem for the town-based population which, for its livelihood, depends upon a clientele derived from the town's traditional sphere of influence. This loss of livelihood for craftsmen and merchants who are unable and unwilling to fall back upon subsistence agriculture has evoked a number of responses. One such response has already been alluded to: the exodus from towns to large cities. The situation, however, is far from that of a treadmill carrying an unsuspecting rural population from tribe to village to town to the big city.

Interesting and important responses are observed in those who remain in towns and villages heavily affected by a decline in economic opportunity.

For those merchants, craftsmen, professional persons, and laborers who reside in, and work out of, fixed facilities within towns economically affected by the loss of a traditional rural hinterland, strategy is employed to free their activities from the limitations of fixed residences. One of the most effective responses involves a shift to itinerancy of activities normally restricted to the town and dependent upon an area of demand. This shift to itinerancy is employed as a mode of strategy to seek out new spheres of influence, to capture a wider consumer area in the absence of a traditional consumer attraction to goods and services based in a moribund economic structure—the town.

For many townsmen dependent upon marketing commodities and services, the threshold of minimum demand necessary for survival cannot be realized without spatially altering their range of operation. Stine (1962), in a study of Korean periodic marketing, defines elements of maximum and minimum ranges which determine the level of success of marketeers considered as firms. These observations are instructive in understanding the conditions under which shifts to itinerancy occur. A maximum range is the range within which consumers are willing to purchase, beyond which is zero demand. The minimum range is the area of demand just large enough to secure success of the firm. When the maximum range is less than the minimum range, a given firm or activity will be forced to become mobile or it will not survive (Stine, 1962:73-74).

The diminishing regional importance of market towns referred to in this discussion can be viewed in terms of these and other considerations. The loss of a town's traditional rural hinterland or sphere of influence often is the result of the changing focus of the consumers' maximum range. Improved transportation routes and lower transportation costs not only increase the maximum range, but, from the point of view of the market town, also bypasses traditional nearby loci of goods and services. In this sense, the maximum range does not shrink, leaving the market town beyond the point of zero demand, but changes its shape, expanding to both bypass the town and to forge new associations with settlements higher in the urban hierarchy. The maximum range of the consumer is also sensitive to the elasticity of demand. As elasticity becomes greater, the maximum range lessens. When traditional goods and services are offered in places closer to the consumer than the market town, such as in the village, and if the consumer is willing to substitute these goods and services for those originally sought after in the town, then the maximum range is shorter. The market town loses a traditional economic sphere of influence due to two processes: *a)* a new fusion of field and center occurs above the settlement level of the town, resulting in the partial abandonment of the town by villagers in need of traditional goods and services; and *b)* many retail and service functions become newly located in villages, negating the economic centripetal forces the town traditionally exerted upon its hinterland.

When these two processes intensify, firms or economic enterprises experience an alteration in the minimum range necessary to secure their success (Stine, 1962:77). The maximum range is a function of the nature of demand density and of the profit level regarded as sufficient for the entrepreneur. A loss or decrease in clientele for commodities or services elicits a variety of responses from individuals as diversified as merchants, professionals, craftsmen, and laborers. Strategy is employed to find new markets and new consumer areas where there is sufficient periodic or continuous demand for their goods and services.

As mentioned above, one striking response to changing economic conditions in such towns is to place any activity amenable to itinerancy on that basis. As migrants and itinerants, individuals, still town-based in residence, are able to syncretize factors of time and space by adjusting their movements to periodic demands. For example, unskilled labor, unable to obtain employment within the town or region, seeks work as diversified as agricultural labor in cotton fields or portering in large cities. Craftsmen such as carpenters, blacksmiths, and masons become mobile, no longer marketing their skills from fixed workshops in one town but, when necessary, traveling to distant towns where their services are needed. Many, however, are able to readily adapt their mode of operation to the periodic market system, traveling on a fixed cycle to as many market places as necessary. Traditionally town-based retailers, such as grocers, grain sellers, green grocers, clothiers, and shoe salesmen, have in many cases converted their stores to depots and, with their inventory, have entered the market circuit as itinerants.

Changes in strategy from fixed to mobile are possible for many; however, for the majority, an entire shift in livelihood is required. Changes in the occupational structure of many towns declining in economic importance are, in large measure, responses to two interrelated factors: significant developments in

Turkey's national economy and attendant changes in local consumption norms. Whereas some town-based occupational forms have declined in the last two decades alone, there has been a meteoric increase in yet others. Changes most greatly affecting the occupational structure in the type of market town discussed here can be considered briefly in the categories of retailing (foodstuffs and nonfood items) and services.

Fixed food retailers in towns have been affected by the abrupt increase in retail services located in villages. Grocery stores, bakeries, coffeehouses, restaurants, mills, wholesalers, and other businesses have opened in villages, obviating the need for villagers to frequent similar businesses in towns. In addition, for large purchases for weddings and other ceremonials, for wholesale purchases by village retailers, and for an array of specialized manufactured consumer goods, villagers are bypassing the intermediate towns for larger urban centers now more accessible to them. Among itinerant marketeers can be found ex-grocers, butchers, and the like who can no longer operate out of a fixed facility in a town.

Retailers of dry goods, construction materials, and a host of other commodities are also affected by competition with similar businesses in larger towns which have more stock and variety to offer than smaller-scale enterprises. In addition, dry goods retailers in fixed shops compete with the torrent of itinerant marketeers who, once a week or more, traditionally inundate the town on its market day. Many of these retailers are forced to join itinerant marketeers on some days of the week to supplement an insufficient income.

Perhaps most severely affected are those townsmen offering services. A number of town-based craftsmen find that their service or commodity is no longer marketable, regardless of mode of marketing, within the town or within wider consumer areas. Most striking examples are cobblers, saddlemakers, potters, tinners, ironmongers, barbers, tailors, and cloth dyers, to name but a few. Developments in the national economy have effectively replaced many traditional locally produced goods with manufactured items.

To cite some examples, town tailors have experienced such competition with factory-made garments as to cause many to shift their activities from the making of suits, shirts, underwear, etc., to the repair of such items, effecting a decline in their income. Many tailors subsequently seek customers as itinerants. Potters cannot compete with comparably-styled factory-made plastic wares retailed by grocers and itinerant marketeers. Few cloth and yarn dyers remain due in part to the ease with which factory-dyed yarn and material may be obtained and to a related decrease in the local production of yarn. Tinners find increasingly fewer customers wishing to have copperwares retinned because aluminum wares are coming to replace items such as copper vessels for cooking. Ironmongers do more repairing of factory-made implements than manufacturing of such items in their forges. Many of these craftsmen for whom a once valuable craft skill has ceased to provide an income have turned to other occupations—occupations which can draw from wider consumer areas than their previous ones. As in the case of retailing functions, villagers able to offer traditional town services in a village setting are turning their proximity to rural consumers to their advantage. The rise within the village of skilled labor and personal services has precluded the need for their town-based counterparts.

In the face of a narrowing base of economic alternatives, the high incidence of cartage indicates the means employed by many to gain an income outside of certain towns. In the ten year period of 1957 to 1967, one town with a 4,500 population, which has severely been affected by a loss of regional importance, showed an increase in automobiles from three to fourteen, microbuses from zero to fourteen, and stake-sided trucks of up to nine tons from eight to fifty-three. These vehicles, representing large investments financed through multiple ownership, are used to derive an income through the hauling of freight and passengers in a wide region which generally does not include the town itself. The owners, drivers, drivers' assistants, and mechanics maintain residence in the town while obtaining income, as do their itinerant marketeer counterparts, from a wide service area.

The activities mentioned—cartage, periodic trading in market places, and migrant forms of skilled and unskilled labor—are the main responses to a failing town economy in the area under consideration. The moribund economy of this type of town is, in many cases, the result of rural affluence. Market towns referred to in this discussion were historically important because of a regional structure in which political power, cultural leadership, and agents of capital were concentrated in the town, effecting an impress upon the region. The bypassing of the market town by a burgeoning rural population is in large measure a result of political and economic changes which have distributed factors of authority, capital, and control of land from the hegemony of the town to the village level.

As an alternative strategy for the marketing of goods, services, and general labor, itinerancy takes command of the potential market relationships existing throughout a wide consumer area. If a rising rural affluence and attendant greater mobility of villagers worked toward bringing about the demise of intermediate market towns, the same factors provide a vision of profit for those individuals who are compelled to reach beyond the confines of the town for a livelihood.

It seems shortsighted to view marketeers and other highly mobile entrepreneurs solely as agents of needed items and finance. It seems even more restrictive to view their behavior merely as adaptive to a given market ecology of "shared poverty." Those involved in itinerant retailing do respond, in part, to real spatial problems of the region in seeking to bring a product or service from a point of origin to a place where buyers can effectively, in terms of time and distance costs, enter into a transaction. It is precisely because of market imperfections resulting from activities which are spatially and temporally separated that marketeers can profit by engaging in arbitrage as a stratagem. More important perhaps is that the lure of profit-taking encourages marketeers to create new resources, new demands, introduce new skills and seek in general to create new market relationships where they did not exist before. Marketeers are agents of information, innovation, and persuasion. Their existence reflects the actual needs of producers and consumers within a given market environment. Because of their existence and through the ability to perceive dimensions of the market, they create new types of producers, consumers and market relations. The ability to perceive potential markets and potential separations of time, space, and demand allows the itinerant agent to be something more than a reactor to the demands of producers and consumers.

The statement has been made, regarding periodic market trade in emerging economies, that these exchange systems are somehow adaptive to a set of conditions which are largely economic. The connotations of the word "adaptive" make it an unfortunate choice to characterize the rationale behind itinerant retailing. Due to a focus upon distributive activities only insofar as these activities meet actual or already existing consumer and producer demands, inadequate concepts of "market" and "marketing" have come to dominate much of the literature. Employing these limited concepts makes it difficult to treat issues such as choice-making by entrepreneurs who are pursuing an expansive policy and who actively work on actualizing potential market relationships rather than merely satisfying existing ones.

Every market is made from two elements: separation and relationship between producers and consumers (McInnes, 1964:56). The separation stems, in part, from the various means by which demand is separated from supply, customers from producers, and increasing wants from an everwidening division of labor. The relations which exist in markets are real in that they can be realized or actualized. In this sense, the market consists of potential relations which are actualized in transactions when an active force perceives and employs elements to generate an exchange. This force is the active process of marketing; individuals seeking to turn a potential market relationship into a real contact.

In short,

Marketing is any "motion" or activity that actualizes the potential relation of producer and consumer. The essential task of marketing is, therefore, always related primarily to the market. The work of marketing always begins with the discovery of market potential (McInnes, 1964:57).

Marketing is not adaptive to existing conditions in any restrictive sense, but rather operates with the market potential inherent in every market. The more pronounced the separation between producer and consumer in terms of space, time, and perception, the greater the market as a source of opportunity.

For the townsmen described in this discussion, itinerancy is a highly successful method for making capital of spatial, temporal, and perceptual separations both actual and created by the entrepreneur. Brief mention of each of these three modes of separation suggested by McInnes (1964:57ff) can stress their value as both obstacle and opportunity.

One function of exchange systems is to forge a closure between activities which are *spatially* separated. Marketing activities such as assembly, transportation, and dispersal seek to bring a product or service from a point of origin to a place where buyers can effectively, in terms of time and distance costs, enter into a transaction. Marketeers operate within a spatial system where factors such as widely dispersed loci of low volume production, extreme regional variation in product and poor transportation and communication networks are but a few obstacles to overcome. Indeed, these factors serve as gain for the marketeer who, through arbitrage, closes the physical separations in the market. In many cases, previously nonexistent spatial problems can be purposely created for the purpose of profit-taking. The stimulation of demand for goods and services spatially distant from consumers where such demand had not previously existed is one such way to open or create a new market separation.

Because marketing is a process in time as well as space, problems arising from the *temporal* separation of desire and availability are resolved through mechanisms and features of marketing. One mechanism is an aspect of finance which seeks to actualize a transaction through the use of credit to coincide demand with availability of product. Low capital resources on the part of both buyer and seller, requiring extensive networks of credit relations, requiring agents to break bulk into miniscule quantities, and requiring mechanisms to counter risk, are important features of the marketing process. The marketeer also devises ways to bring about a time lapse in the marketing process which serves to heighten consumers' level of demand, resulting in greater profit. Storage, altering prices upward with the awarding of credit, and adding unrealistic transport costs to the price of goods are some ways in which time is used to the seller's benefit.

Marketeers play an important role as agents of information and persuasion who seek to attract buyers to an area and products and also to reinforce separations between potential buyers and competitors. These market agents are often portrayed in analysis as brokers who seek to align *perceptual differences* between themselves and buyers. They align bid and offer, based upon consideration of offering price and asking price in terms of such things as utility and ability to pay. It is in these areas that marketeers can manipulate consumers, bringing them, through information and persuasion, to desire new products and services. Various techniques are employed to inform and direct buyers to specific products and to widen the gap between the sellers' knowledge of product quality and price and the buyers' concept of the same. Throughout, the marketeer treads between the desire to take a high profit margin as a means of countering risks involved in marketing and the necessity to maintain and cultivate a reputation which will continue to attract a clientele to his goods and services.

The search for market potentials and the necessity of placing their activities on a mobile basis are complementary for townsmen required to search for economic alternatives beyond the economically moribund confines of the town. The rural periodic market systems which reflect their strategies are not totally adaptive to a given market environment. Rather, depending upon their perception of dimensions of the market, marketeers work in terms of potential as well as actual markets.

A CONSIDERATION OF INTERREGIONAL EXCHANGE IN GREATER MESOPOTAMIA: 4000-3000 B.C.

Henry T. Wright

INTRODUCTION

ARCHAEOLOGISTS have long attempted to understand extinct interregional economies by studying the distribution of distinctive artifacts in areas removed from their locus of production. More often than not, these attempts have involved defining the period during which a product was repeatedly transported and mapping the region within which it was distributed. Such studies only demonstrate the existence and spread of trade networks; they provide neither elucidation of the mechanics of interregional exchange nor tests for the explanation of various cultural developments in terms of changing exchange networks.

To achieve these two purposes, it is useful to estimate the values of different commodities at different points in the network and the volume of transport between such points. Changes in both the value of different commodities (cf. Winters, 1968) and the volume transported (cf. Renfrew, Dixon, and Cann, 1969) can indicate the social context and regulatory controls of exchange. In addition, correlations between changing volumes of transported commodities and other variables can lead to the rejection or acceptance of possible explanations of cultural development. In this paper I shall attempt to use such estimates to test whether or not state development and population growth are explained by increased exchange.[1]

Two categories of network studies are definable. One involves the consideration of transport through a single node in a network for a period of time. The other involves consideration of transport through two or more nodes in a network. In either case, the archaeological data used are observations on discarded artifacts at a site. Moreover, the artifact samples must be

---

[1] This is a total revision of a paper presented at the 1969 Annual meeting of the American Anthropological Association in New Orleans. The changes result in part from the constructive comments of my friends, whom I thank, and in part from a complete reexamination of the body of data from Farukhabad.

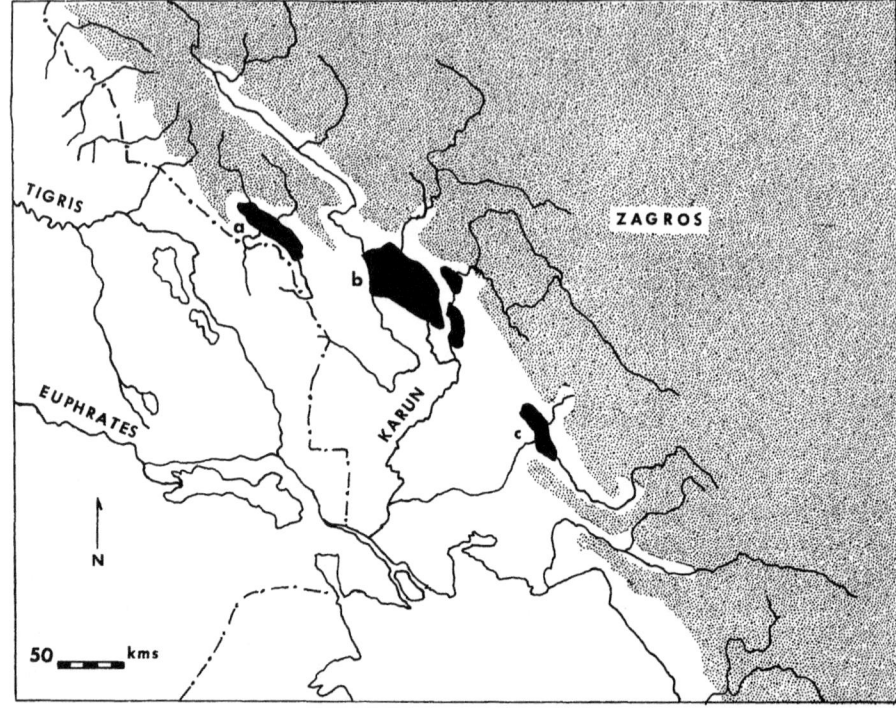

Fig. 1. The Central Zagros. The stippled area is rugged land above 800 m. The black areas are the major settled plains of southwestern Iran:
  a The Deh Luran Plain and Tepe Farukhabad
  b The Susiana Plain
  c The Ram Hormuz Plain

representative of those in the site or sites, and the assumptions which one makes in order to derive measures of exchange variables from the data must be explicit. Clearly, in order to study two or more sites one must have comparable samples from these sites. Such comparability is rare. It is therefore seldom possible even to test such simple hypotheses as "the value of a commodity is a function of transport distance from the source" or "volume of a commodity moving through a point is a function of the population served by that part of the network beyond this point." In this paper, only one node will be considered.

AN EXCHANGE NETWORK

To exemplify an approach using data from a single node, let us consider a small, fourth millennium B.C. center in Greater

Mesopotamia. Given the technology of the period, Greater Mesopotamia can be divided into three major material resource zones (Fig. 1). In the center is the Tigris-Euphrates alluvium. This was an area of high subsistence potential lacking stones, metals, large timber, and many other resources. North of this are the folded and eroded Zagros Mountains, rich in cherts for stone cutting tools, gypsum and limestone for stone containers, and timber. Seepages of bitumen, useful as an adhesive and waterproofing, occur along the juncture of these two zones. North and east of the Zagros are the Anatolian Plateau, Iranian Plateau, and the basins and ranges of Baluchistan and Afghanistan. In these occur metals, cherts, igneous rocks for durable ground stone artifacts, and gems for ornaments. As one moves from the alluvium through the rugged mountains to the poorly watered plateau, both settlement size and the size of inhabited enclaves drop. There were a limited number of routes and methods for moving resources from the thinly populated and relatively material-rich plateau to the densely populated and relatively material-poor alluvium. The mountains had to be crossed by one of a number of tracks, carrying goods on human backs or perhaps pack animals. Upon reaching the foot of the mountains, lateral movement by river boats or gulf sailing crafts was possible.

The center to be considered is Tepe Farukhabad on the Deh Luran Plain of Southwest Iran. Limited excavations were conducted here in 1968 by a team from the University of Michigan Museum of Anthropology and the Iran Archaeological Service.[2] The Deh Luran Plain was one of the small, settled enclaves south of the higher ridges of the Zagros but within the first low folds of the ranges. It is about one hundred kilometers westnorthwest of the similar but much larger Susiana Plain and about one hundred kilometers north of the heartland of Tigris-Euphrates alluvium. Several of the possible routes between these two densely populated areas passed through the Deh Luran Plain. In addition to its location, the plain had the advantage of a number of useful resources. On the northeast edge of the plain is a large bitumen seepage. Immediately to the north of the plain, the ridges rise above one thousand meters in altitude, and even today oak is relatively plentiful. On the southeast end of the plain is an extensive granular chert source. Throughout the area, gypsum and calcite boulders occur. All of these materials

---

[2] These excavations were supported by National Science Foundation Grant GS-1936.

were collected and brought to the settlement at Farukhabad near the southwest edge of the plain.

The history of Farukhabad is now well documented. This settlement was founded before 5000 B.C. By the late 'Ubaid Period, about 4000 B.C., it was a small center with both simple and elaborate buildings, probably very similar to a number of other settlements on the plain. After an abandonment of several centuries, the site was reoccupied near the end of the Early Uruk Period. By the Late Uruk Period it had once again grown into a small center with both simple and elaborate buildings. It was probably the only such center on the thinly occupied plain. During the Jemdet Nasr Period, about 3000 B.C., this small center was subsidiary to a large town in the center of the plain. Farukhabad was abandoned during the later Early Dynastic Period, but it was periodically reoccupied until the first millennium A.D.

Farukhabad has been cut in half by the nearby Memeh River. Given the time and resources at our disposal, I decided to sample along this convenient transect through the site. Two five-by-five-meter blocks were arbitrarily selected along this face. In retrospect, it is likely that this method will result in a bias for the smaller central area of the site which probably had larger, more elaborate buildings. For this reason, we cannot estimate absolute consumption of either imports or local products. As the blocks were excavated down the face, all occupational refuse was screened with a standard 5mm mesh.

EXPORTS AND IMPORTS

To be useful in a quantitative study, an export from an archaeologically documented settlement must be relatively common. It must also leave both some evidence of production independent of the discarded finished artifact and the discarded artifacts themselves. An increase in export can only be measured by comparing increase in production with increase in consumption. Several examples illustrate this point. Utilization of oak is indicated by rare occurrences of charcoal which could be either burned discarded artifacts or burned waste. Thus it is not useful. Since utilization of calcite and gypsum is indicated almost exclusively by discarded finished grinding stones and stone bowls, they are not useful. In the case of chert utilization, both core-trimming flakes, cores, and finished tools are present, but there is no evidence that the various types of chert from Deh Luran were exported. However, in the case of bitumen there are several distinctive by-products of manufacture and there are distinctive artifacts. Bitumen preserves well at the site. It proves to be a useful measure of export.

The bitumen seepage near Farukhabad has laid down layer upon layer of rock asphalt mixed with sediment and fragments of plants. This material is much easier to mine than the tenacious semiliquid fresh bitumen. Blocks of rock asphalt were returned to Tepe Farukhabad, and many fragments were discarded without any further treatment. These blocks can be heated until the foreign matter floats or sinks from the bitumen. The cleaned bitumen can be either packaged in a container for export or used locally. There were a very limited number of local uses. Cracked ceramic vessels were patched. Chert sickle blades were mounted in wooden handles. Reed and pole matting probably used in houses was sometimes coated with bitumen. At various times small bitumen spheres, perforated ovoids, and other items were made and discarded. The two major uses for bitumen in alluvial Mesopotamia, as architectural water-proofing and as boat caulking, are not attested in Deh Luran. Given the small and seasonal character of the local rivers, boats would have had little utility. The large amount of waste bitumen, both rock asphalt and melted pieces, relative to artifacts must reflect the differential demand and consequent high, though varying, export production.[3]

To be useful in a quantitative study of exchange, an import into a settlement must be common, and there must be some way to measure variation in import independent of variation resulting from use for different purposes. Many of the imports to Farukhabad are too rare for use in a quantitative study. Among these are obsidian, copper, basalt, marine shell, carnelian, and lapis lazuli. A common import is high quality chert. This is frequently used along with local chert for all blade tools except sickle blades. A local coarse gray chert is preferred for these. Variability resulting from different uses can be controlled by considering only one tool category. In this study, retouched and utilized blades and blade segments which were probably used for a variety of cutting activities are considered. The relative value of the import chert can be calculated on the assumption that local chert, being obtained and worked in the same manner through time, has a constant value. Given constant exports, a

---

[3] A chemical study of bitumen samples from Farukhabad and other sites is now being conducted by Dr. Robert Marschner with the support of the American Oil Company. The study is hampered by our inability to obtain samples from the many seepages in Iraq and Syria.

decrease in the proportion of import chert to some constant amount of local chert indicates increase in the exchange value of the imports, and vice versa.

We have considered both some general problems of imported and exported commodities in archaeological contexts and some characteristics of the specific materials found at Farukhabad. Now let us examine the participation of a single node in greater Mesopotamian exchange networks during the fourth millennium.

FOURTH MILLENNIUM EXCHANGE DEVELOPMENTS

Data on objects of different materials are presented in the accompanying tables.[4] We will examine each phase in turn.

The Farukh Phase, a stylistically distinct Deh Luran manifestation of the Late 'Ubaid Period, is our base point. Table 1 shows that in the total amount of screened Farukh Phase refuse, there were 35 grams of bitumen waste per cubic meter and 5 grams of bitumen spheres, bitumen-covered mat fragments, lashings, etc. Table 2 shows that major bitumen production could occur in either simple or elaborate buildings. There was no monopoly on production. On the other hand, stone for chipped tools was the only common class of import. For every 10 blades of local chert, there were 7 of exotic chert. In addition, small quantities of obsidian were being introduced. There were few other imports.

In the succeeding Early Uruk to Early Jemdet Nasr Periods, bitumen production, as indicated by waste density, fluctuated at a low level, while the utilized bitumen artifacts consistantly declined. Note however that there are so few artifacts that even if the manufacture of each artifact left twice its weight in waste, the trends in bitumen waste density would hardly be affected by this apparent decrease in use. On the other hand, for every ten blades of local chert, we found only one or two blades of imported chert. The value of these stones had more than tripled relative to their Farukh Phase value. Thus there was relatively constant local production, but the value of previously easily-obtained commodities rose, since so few of them reached Deh Luran. The Late 'Ubaid exchange network was no longer effectively supplying Deh Luran.

During the Early Uruk to Early Jemdet Nasr Phases there is evidence that the exchange network was undergoing a trans-

---

[4]These figures are subject to minor revisions before final publication of the Farukhabad Report.

Table 1

LOCAL AND NONLOCAL MATERIALS AT TEPE FARUKHABAD

Period	Total Cubic Meters Screened	Grams Waste Bitumen/ M³	Number Bitumen Tools	Grams Bitumen Tools/ M³	Local Chert Blades	Non-Local Chert Blades	Ratio Local: Import	Obsidian	Copper	Basalt	Marine Shell	Carnelian	Lapis Lazuli
Late Jemdet Nasr	27	252	8	15.8	41	17	10:4		1	9	11		4
Early Jemdet Nasr	44	31	3	.4	95	14	10:2		1	2	5	2	
Late Uruk	26	60	5	2.2	127	16	10:1	1			5	1	
Early-Middle Uruk	37	20	5	3.2	74	15	10:2	2	2		1		
Farukh	63	35	14	5.3	144	109	10:7	2					

Table 2

BITUMEN DENSITY IN SIMPLE (S) AND ELABORATE (E)
BUILDINGS AT FARUKHABAD

Period	No.	Type	Excavation	Feature	Layer	M^3 Screened	Grams Bitumen Waste	Grams Bitumen/ M^3
Late Jemdet Nasr								
	1	S	B	10AB	21-19	7.8	402	51
	2	E	A	1DC	10-6	8.3	2589	312
	3	E	B	10CB	23-22	10.0	4084	408
Early Jemdet Nasr								
	4	S	A	12B	17-14	8.2	231	28
	5	S	A	12A	13 L-M	3.6	25	7
	6	S	A	15	18	3.3	30	9
	7	E	A	1E	12-11	5.4	98	18
	8	E	A	1F	13 U	2.3	66	28
	9	E	B	10DC	26-24	13.8	806	58
Late Uruk								
	10	S	A	16	19	2.7	5	2
	11	S	A	20-22	21	4.8	71	15
	12	E	B	22-23	31U-30	6.7	491	73
Middle Uruk								
	13	S	B	26	33U	3.9	44	11
Early Uruk								
	14	S	B	37	36	6.4	318	50
Farukh								
	15	S	B	40	41	6.5	223	34
	16	S	B	41	44	4.1	15	4
	17	E	A	25	30-31	1.5	48	32
	18	E	A	28-29	27-24	14.5	231	16
	19	E	A	30	23-22	2.7	103	38

formation. Obsidian was no longer transported, but such technically useful materials as copper and vesicular basalt and such socially useful materials as marine shell and carnelian appear, even in our small sample. These shifts in minor commodities suggest decreased exchange with northern Iraq and increased exchange with central Iran and the Gulf area. Until the sources of copper, basalt, and carnelian can be identified, this possible change in territorial orientation cannot be verified. Whatever the explanation of these shifts, these and other evidences suggest that a new exchange network was growing up around the large Uruk Period towns of alluvial Mesopotamia and the Susiana Plain. However, the Deh Luran Plain does not appear to have participated significantly in this new network.

Examination of Table 2 suggests that from Late Uruk times onward there was more bitumen waste in elaborate buildings than in small buildings. This may indicate that production for export was concentrated in these structures. Such a conclusion cannot be accepted unless it is shown that this larger amount of waste cannot be explained by an increased bitumen tool use in these buildings. This is not now possible given the small samples of bitumen tools.

In the Late Jemdet Nasr Period, there were major changes. There was an overall eight-fold increase in bitumen density to 250 grams per cubic meter, resulting from a three-fold increase in waste density for simple buildings and a ten-fold increase in waste density in elaborate buildings. There were 16 grams of bitumen tools per cubic meter. Unfortunately the proportional increase in export production cannot be estimated because we do not have large enough tool samples to accurately estimate changes in local consumption. On the other hand, for every ten blades of local chert there were four of exotic chert or an approximate doubling in their relative use. In addition, there was marked increase in other, less common import commodities such as basalt, marine shell, and semiprecious stone. Since local bitumen production increased so radically, this increase in imports need not be explained as a result of decreases in their relative value. The increase in imports could be more reasonably explained as a result of an increase in exports. If so, by Late Jemdet Nasr times the Deh Luran area had considerably increased its participation in the transformed exchange network that developed during the Uruk Period.

In summary, this consideration of the occurrence of various types of materials at Farukhabad indicated a simple Late 'Ubaid exchange network in which few commodities were transported in any quantity. During the succeeding Uruk period this simple network did not adequately supply the Deh Luran Plain with high quality chert. Also, during this period there are indications of a change in the organization of local production of bitumen and indications of a change in the kinds of commodities transported. During the Late Jemdet Nasr Period, Deh Luran was apparently integrated into a transformed network in which large quantities of many commodities were transported.

INTERREGIONAL EXCHANGE, THE STATE, AND POPULATION GROWTH

For the purposes of this paper, a state is defined as a sociocultural system with a specialized administrative subsystem. In Mesopotamia its existence is indicated by an administrative technology including official seals, number systems, and special buildings. At Farukhabad, a numbered and sealed *bulla* was found in later Middle Uruk layers. Since only the small center of Farukhabad and a few villages occupied the plain at this time, it is likely that the Deh Luran Plain was a marginal part of a larger state centered somewhere else, probably on the Susiana Plain. If so, the Deh Luran area was drawn into a state long before it participated significantly in the transformed exchange network. The latter cannot explain the former.

Population increase and population nucleation are indicated by growth in the number and size of settlements. On the Deh Luran Plain, settlement reached a nadir during the Middle and Late Uruk periods. During the Jemdet Nasr period however most centers, large and small, were reoccupied. By Late Jemdet Nasr times all were occupied and population was perhaps double its Farukh Phase level. It seems that the major population growth preceeded major participation in the new exchange network. If so, the latter cannot explain the former.

Thus there is one likely case against the hypothesis that interregional exchange alone causes either state development or what is commonly called urbanism. Furthermore, it seems as fruitful to pursue some contrary ideas: that state development implies both changed demand for goods and changed political geography which require changes in the pattern of interregional exchange and that population growth stimulates increased volume of exchange.

CONCLUSION

I hope that this example demonstrates the utility of quantitative archaeological studies of exchange. Let me recapitulate some of the pitfalls. First, one should have equivalent recovery procedures in each area sampled. Screened samples of a waste product from here and hand-picked samples from there would be misleading. Second, one should have samples representative of the sites being studied. If samples are biased, then some attempt must be made to account for this in analysis. Third, one has to devise some means of measuring import and export independent of local use. The means will differ in various research situations. In the above example, local consumption of the export commodity was minor and the density of the waste product could have been used as an indicator of export for the immediate objective. However, even with small samples of bitumen tools, a rough assessment of the contribution of increased local consumption was possible. However, exact correction would require not only larger samples but also knowledge of the absolute amount of waste created in the manufacture of each bitumen tool type. On the other hand, import cherts had to be estimated relative to local inferior substitutes in the above example. The absolute amount of import chert could have been estimated if we had a representative sample from the site, since all the import material would sooner or later have been discarded.

I originally set out to consider the relation between interregional exchange and both state development and demographic growth in a portion of Greater Mesopotamia. The major increase in participation in interregional exchange occurred during the Jemdet Nasr Period. This is in keeping with the evidence from other nearby areas. Though the evidence is slim, and can perhaps be interpreted in ways other than that presented above, it seems that the state as a political form developed prior to this increased participation in exchange. In addition, major demographic changes seem to have begun before increased participation in exchange. These results suggest that the explanation of the rise of the state and the growth of great population centers is to be sought in variables other than increasing volume of interregional exchange.

A CULTURAL ADAPTIVE APPROACH TO MALAGASY POLITICAL ORGANIZATION[1]

Conrad P. Kottak

ANTHROPOLOGISTS are familiar with societal and cultural typologies which group noncontiguous, nonrelated human populations on the basis of certain analogous structural features, behavioral patterns and cultural traits. Typologies labeled "evolutionary" by those who have proposed them have been formulated by Fried (1959), Service (1962), and Steward (1955) among others. Fried's types are "egalitarian," "ranked," "stratified," and "state-organized" societies. Service's types are called "band," "tribe," "chiefdom," and "state." These types are essentially those of general evolution as distinguished from specific evolution by Sahlins and Service (1960). Ecological variables are not important in their definitions.

Julian Steward's cross-cultural types, e.g., "patrilineal band," "composite band," "multifamily predatory band," "irrigation state," and others are fundamentally different, as are those cultural adaptive types formulated in this paper, in that they are based on ecological variables. They are intended as means of ordering data so as to demonstrate interrelationships among certain environmental, demographic and social-cultural variables and to suggest hypotheses involving them.

There is, however, a fundamental difference between cross-cultural and cultural adaptive typologies. While Steward's cross-cultural formulations are attempts to delineate and to explain sociocultural similarities which have arisen recurrently and independently among historically, genetically, and geographically unrelated populations, the cultural adaptive formulations of the present paper are concerned with explaining sociocultural differentiation among genetically, historically and geographically related human populations. While Steward has invoked ecological factors to explain sociocultural similarities, I shall be concerned with

---

[1] I wish to thank the Foreign Area Fellowship Program for a postdoctoral field grant which supported part of the research on which this paper is based. I also want to thank Aram Yengoyan for his useful criticisms of an earlier version of this paper.

the role of ecological variables in producing sociocultural differences, in this case in the realm of political organization.

DESCRIPTION OF THE MODEL

A cultural adaptive model such as that employed in this paper is appropriate for studies involving a group of human populations or ethnic units all of which are assumed to be descended from a common ancestral population with a common ancestral culture. *Cultural adaptation* refers to the fact that through time subdivisions of the original population may split off and occupy new environments, some of which may differ markedly from the habitat of the ancestral group. Few anthropologists would dispute the contention that human populations adapt to their environments principally through the sociocultural means at their disposal. When the environment changes, or when a new environment is occupied, the cultural adaptive kit of the population prior to the change may be modifed. There are several potential sources of raw material for sociocultural adaptation to the new environment techniques and behavior patterns may be borrowed from other ethnic units; ancestral sociocultural forms may be modifed; traits of the protoculture may be rearranged or recombined; the functions of ancestral forms may change; or entirely new cultural adaptive means may be independently invented.

Finally, it is important to stress that components of the environment to which a given human population adapts consist not only of those variables which any anthropologist would readily call "ecological," e.g., flora, fauna, climatic features and soil types, but also variables involving other human groups which may be competing for the same resources, may be providing outlets for certain local products, or may be supplying raw materials. In Madagascar, for example, the cultural adaptive model would be of very limited utility if it tried to explain the existenc of certain sociocultural phenomena with reference only to the local ecosystem of a given Malagasy population. Sociocultural forms reflect the involvement of human populations in regional and interethnic as well as in local subsistence ecosystems.

My use of a cultural adaptive model to study sociocultural variation is not new. Ecological variables have been used to explain cultural adaptive radiation and differentiation among historically related human populations by several scholars, cf., Sahlins (1958); Gulliver (1955); Steward et al. (1956). Goodenough (1955) has offered a reconstruction of ancestral forms of Malayo-

Polynesian kinship and descent systems and has discussed formal
changes in these common ancestral institutions among daughter
populations. The analogy of the cultural adaptive model in ethnology to the comparative method in linguistics is also noted.

MADAGASCAR AS A LABORATORY FOR THE STUDY OF CULTURAL ADAPTIVE RADIATION

Madagascar is a particularly good place to study cultural
adaptive radiation because, within a fairly clearly bounded area,
one encounters several populations which are linguistically similar but very diverse in terms of behavior patterns and functioning of institutions. Many of these sociocultural differences may
be viewed as responses to selective pressures associated with
specific environments. The range of natural environments is
broad as this is the world's fourth largest island. Madagascar,
since 1960 the Malagasy Republic, is 1580 kilometers long and
600 kilometers across at its widest point. The island's total
area is 590,000 square kilometers. Its present population is
around six million. The tropical highlands of central Madagascar,
the rainforest of the eastern escarpment, the humid coastal low-
lands of the east, the savannah and bush country of the south and
west, and the alluvial valleys of the southeast coast are only
some of the distinctive environmental areas. Fission and adaptive radiation into contrasting environments must have begun
soon after first settlement of the island, which took place some
2000 years ago. Also facilitating the use of the cultural adaptive model for Madagascar is the fact that, because of the island's
size, those Malagasy ethnic units which have diverged have been
able, to a certain extent, to create and to retain consciousness
of their particular and distinctive ethnic or tribal identities.

Sociocultural differentiation and adaptive radiation in Madagascar can be assessed only after some discussion of cultural
uniformities which are common to all Malagasy. Three of the
most salient reasons for this uniformity in sociocultural forms
are readily discernible. First, all Malagasy speak closely related dialects and languages differentiated from a common Western Indonesian protolanguage spoken some 2000 years ago (Vérin,
Kottak, and Gorlin, 1970). Second, beginning in the seventeenth
century, previously distinct and autonomous Malagasy populations
have been welded into political confederations and states, which
have enforced common behavior patterns and institutions upon
populations living within their territorial limits. The expansion

of the Merina state of the northcentral highlands during the nineteenth century did much to produce uniformity in those areas under its control. Finally, French rule of Madagascar, which was established in 1896 and ended in 1960 also promoted pan-Malagasy uniformity. The nature of French influence in Madagascar lies beyond the scope of the present paper. The first two reasons for similarities encountered among Malagasy populations will receive more detailed attention.

THE HERITAGE OF THE PROTO-MALAGASY

I refer to the first human settlers of Madagascar as the proto-Malagasy. They are assumed to have been part of a group of Indonesian traders who ultimately arrived in Madagascar after following an Indian Ocean trade route which included ports of the East African coast. In the absence of written documentation and because serious archaeological work has begun in Madagascar only during the past decade, the outline of the early settlement and history of the island is tentative at best. Maximum linguistic diversity is encountered in the north and northwest, suggesting the northern coasts as the area of original settlement. A glottochronological study (Vérin, Kottak and Gorlin, 1970) suggests that population spread down the east and west coasts, with divergence of western and eastern subgroups having taken place around the seventh century A.D. Subdivisions of the west coast population gradually moved inland as cattle herders, occupying the western interior, the south, and the central highlands. Around A.D. 1300, migrants from the east coast also began to penetrate the interior, bringing with them an agricultural economy based on wet-rice cultivation. Eventually they displaced and absorbed the pastoral populations of the interior and gave rise to the Merina and Betsileo groups (see Fig. 1).

The cultural adaptive model set forth above assumes a single, relatively homogeneous protoculture as a base from which adaptive divergence has taken place. For several reasons it is impossible to know to what extent the Malagasy fulfill this assumption. While there is a marked linguistic uniformity throughout all Malagasy speech communities, the result of the common protolanguage, there is no doubt that the proto-Malagasy cultural heritage has been embellished over the centuries with contributions from several non-Malagasy sources. Madagascar was founded by traders, and economic links with other world areas, most notably with the East African coast, have been maintained throughout Malagasy history, although at times trade has been interrupted or scaled down in volume as new maritime powers have arisen in the western Indian Ocean. Because of this extra-island exchange network, some coastal Malagasy populations have had long histories of direct contact with East Africans. Since the tenth century, Islamic Swahilli-speaking traders have engaged in commerce in Malagasy ports, introducing both Arabic and African contributions to Malagasy culture. In addition to subsequent external influence, there is reason to doubt the purely Indonesian character of the proto-Malagasy character itself. In vocabulary, phenotype and genotype, African contributions to Madagascar are evident. This follows from the assumption that Indonesian traders reached Madagascar after having first established trade contacts with East African ports (Deschamps, 1960).

Regardless of the nature of the protoculture, all Malagasy populations have subsequently been exposed, either directly in the case of coastal Malagasy or indirectly by diffusion from coasts to interior, to cultural influences derived from East Africa and Arabia. Thus, while it is impossible to demonstrate the nature of the protoculture, the cultural adaptive model is still appropriate, since both the protoculture and its later embellishments from non-Malagasy areas have been available to all Malagasy. Through time, both ancestral and borrowed sociocultural forms have been subjected to the screening effects of the diverse environmental niches ultimately filled by the expanding population.

THE HERITAGE OF MERINA RULE

The growth of the Merina state, which by 1850 had approximately two-thirds of the island under its political and administrative control, is another major reason for Malagasy unity. The extension of Merina rule belongs to a tradition of unification through the evolution of states begun by the Sakalava of the west coast. Sakalava expansion involved the incorporation of diverse and previously autonomous descent groups of the west coast and immediate interior into a political confederation. The cause of Sakalava supremacy seems to have been their early and privileged access to European munitions. During the late seventeenth and most of the eighteenth centuries, the Sakalava confederacy was the major political power of Madagascar.

While most Malagasy societies have been organized at some time on at least a chiefdom basis, the major achievement of Malagasy political organization was the Merina state. Formed in the late eighteenth century in the rich rice plain around Tananarive, the present national capital, the Merina state controlled most of Madagascar until the French conquest of the Merina in 1895. By the end of King Radama's reign in 1827, the Merina empire had attained its widest extent of effective political control. Only the pastoral Tandroy and Mahafaly of the south and southwest, parts of the extreme north, and areas of the former Sakalava confederacy of the west remained independent.

The Merina economy was founded on irrigated rice agriculture, manufacturing, and the control of long-distance trade routes. As they expanded, the Merina incorporated under a single rule a variety of the diverse ecological niches of the island. Tananarive, the capital, became the focus for collection and reallocation of products and services; both internal production in the subjugated areas and foreign imports were controlled. A series of military expeditions begun during the reign of King Andrianampoinimerina (1787-1810) and continued under his son Radama I (1810-1827) established Merina control over major ports of the east and west. Duties were collected by Merina bureaucrats on virtually all items imported to Madagascar. The west coast harbors and their commerce, which had formerly provided economic support for Sakalava elites, were controlled by Merina by 1830. After conquering the northern Sakalava province of Boina in 1824, the Merina replaced the Sakalava as collectors of a harbor tax levied on all vessels entering Majunga Bay. These included European ships and dhows from East Africa and the Persian Gulf.

Until the abolition of the external slave trade in 1820, native Malagasy appear to have been the principal export of the Merina state. Various legal codes established by successive rulers of Imerina reduced free Malagasy into slavery for a series of crimes. Exportable slaves were also added through military expeditions. Prisoners of war, members of other Malagasy ethnic units who had resisted Merina rule, became slaves whom the Merina government could exchange for European firearms and other imports on the coasts.

In internal affairs, the capital city of Tananarive became a node of integration and articulation for several different environmental zones. The environmental range open to exploitation by the Merina population was considerably expanded by military expeditions. Imerina itself lacks abundant pasture land, a deficiency overcome with the early addition of a region located to its east and northeast. This level area, between two lines of

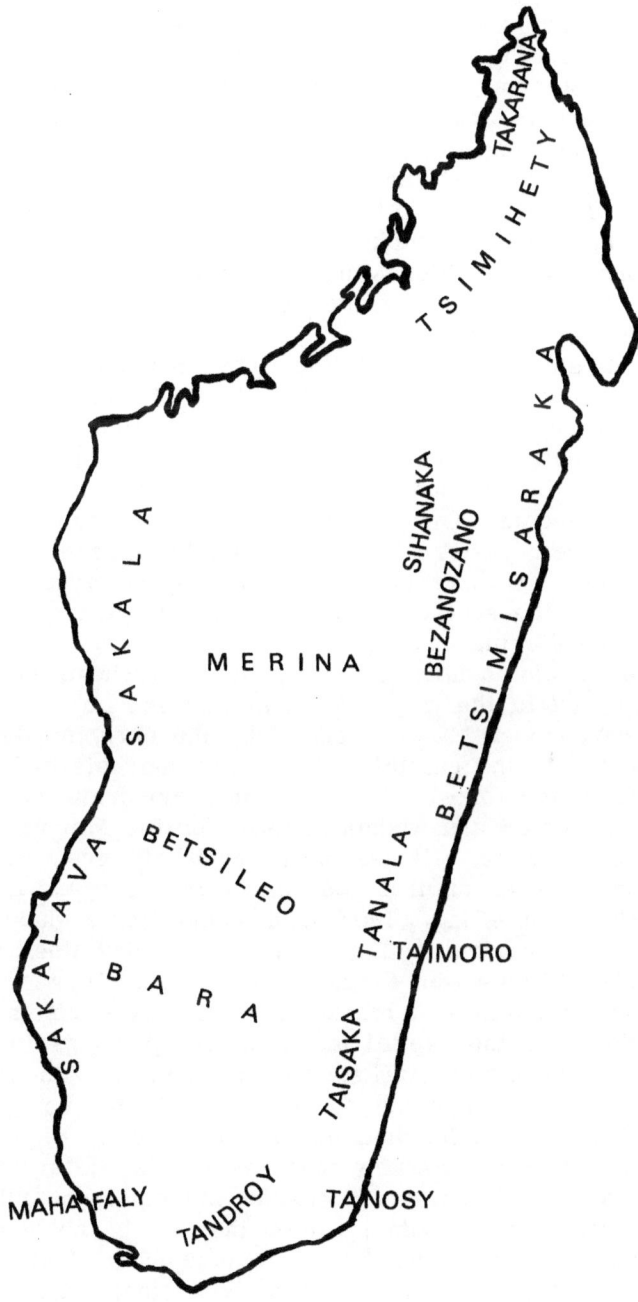

Fig. 1. Location of Malagasy ethnic units.

tropical forest, was the homeland of the Bezanozano and the Sihanaka (see Fig. 1). Following the submission of these ethnic units, the Merina elite sent their cattle herds, stores of their wealth, there to graze. The resources traditionally exploited by the Bezanozano and the Sihanaka were also incorporated into the Merina economy; Sihanaka supplied dried fish from Lake Alaotra as well as basketry products woven from swamp and marsh vegetation around the lake to the capital through a regional marketing system which Merina officials originated and maintained. Sihanaka also traveled on foot to the markets of Imerina to peddle their wares.

In all subjugated areas, the native populations were required to render government service for their Merina overlords. Stockaded provincial outposts of the Merina administration, the sites of market activity dominated by Merina merchants, and seats of the Merina government were constructed with the labor of the conquered people. One of the principal uses which the Merina found for their eastern neighbors, the Bezanozano, was as porters. Bezanozano were prominent in the transport of goods from the highlands to the east coast and of coastal and imported goods back to the Merina capital.

The Tanala, a horticultural population whose homeland is the northern part of the tropical forest between Imerina and the east coast, were under Merina control by the early nineteenth century. Transported to the capital and to other markets of Imerina, hard woods from the forest were made into elaborate coffins for Merina noblemen and wooden houses for the Merina elite. On the forest borders, villages of iron-workers grew in number on sites located near natural sources of iron ore and forest timber necessary to smelting. Iron spades and sickle blades were essential to the agricultural economy of Imerina itself. The Merina state offered protection to these blacksmith villages, and Merina tradesmen guaranteed a market for their products in the highland

Artisans in the capital manufactured products to be distributed through a network of markets which expanded with each conquest of new areas and with the construction of each new provincial town. South of the Merina, among the Betsileo of the southern highlands, the first markets were established after the imposition of Merina rule. Merina merchants, principally members of the *hova* or commoner stratum rather than of the noble or ruling group known as *andriana*, hawked a congeries of Merina manufactured goods, products collected from other parts of Madagascar, and foreign imports. The Merina also introduced the slave market to the Betsileo. The Merina administration in the market town guaranteed the peace of the market and the free movement of people and goods from the countryside.

By ca. 1820 the Merina had extended their influence to the northern part of the territory of the pastoral Bara. Some 100 kilometers south of the Betsileo they established Ihosy as a tradepost and administrative town in Bara country. In exchange for money and beads, Merina obtained cattle from the Bara. Marina military expeditions added the two major ports of southern Madagascar to their growing empire. Fort Dauphin, on the southeast coast, was a commercial center, formerly controlled by the noble lineage of the Tanosy. In the west, Tulear had become the major port of the southern Sakalava.

Throughout their empire, the Merina imposed a single code of laws, though punishments were made only half as severe in recently incorporated parts of the island. Governmental edicts and revisions in the legal code were proclaimed by the sovereign and communicated by his or her representatives to the provincial governors and down through a hierarchy of officials who administered the conquered areas. The Merina state subjected all its people to often onerous taxation, corvee labor and other forms of harassment.

Merina incorporation of other Malagasy ethnic units was often facilitated by alliances between Merina rulers and branches of chiefly families in the provinces. In return for their cooperation, the Merina rewarded these nobles with access to wealth and power beyond anything they had previously enjoyed. Among the Betsileo, for example, prior to Merina rule there had been two major states and several minor chiefdoms competing for supremacy. An alliance between the Merina king and the noble lineage of one of these states raised the latter to a position of power and preeminence over all Betsileo which would have been impossible for him to gain without external support.

The economic foundations of the Merina state have been discussed at length because of the contrast between the Merina and other Malagasy populations to be considered below. The Merina created one of the largest and most cohesive states of the tropics. When considering Malagasy ethnic units, one should not overlook the impact of the Merina state in the production of common denominators in Malagasy culture. One should not assume that he is observing pristine tribal societies when he is, in fact, dealing with populations who have been subjected to over 100 years of foreign rule by nation states, first Merina, then France. In my own field study of the Betsileo, for example, I found that many behavior patterns and conceptualizations characteristic of contemporary Betsileo life had their origin under Merina rule. The Merina state was also responsible for the termination of internecine warfare in many of its provinces. Pax Merina allowed trade and interethnic contacts to take place on an unprecedented level.

It is not, however, sufficient simply to understand that certain common denominators and interethnic contacts were the results of Merina rule. More important is the fact that Merina rule was responsible for the very creation of many of the contemporary Malagasy ethnic units. The official census currently divides the population of the Malagasy Republic into twenty *ethnies,* translated throughout this paper as "ethnic units." They are located on Figure 1. The census of the French colonial administration in Madagascar employed the same ethnic labels. However, many of these names do not appear on a list of Malagasy societies published by Flacourt in 1661, prior to the formation and expansion of the Merina state. Many of these ethnic labels were, in fact, products of Merina expansion. The Betsileo for example, constituted no bounded or self-conscious kind of unit prior to their conquest by the Merina. Nor, in the absence of the political cohesion provided by a single territorial administration, did the pre-Merina Betsileo have any kinship basis for unity. No common genealogy links all Betsileo or even the noble lineages of the once independent political subdivisions.[2]

Thus, one must recognize that fortuitous and political factors have been instrumental in forming many Malagasy ethnic units. Consider for example, the distinction between the Betsileo and the Bara, their neighbors to the south and west. Most Betsileo live in the highlands as peasant cultivators of wet rice. As one moves south and west, however, temperatures rise, rainfall diminishes, and sources of water for irrigation become scarce. Cattle herding becomes more and more important, and rice is gradually replaced by maize, manioc and other crops. As one travels through this country, if he wishes to know where the Betsileo stop and the Bara begin, he will usually have to ask someone. There is a gradual, ecotonal transition in cultural adaptation. The distinction between these two units appears to have been created by the Merina when they drew an administrative line between the Betsileo province, with its capital at Fianarantsoa, and the Bara province, with its capital at Ihosy. Through time, this administrative division has come to be regarded as an

---

[2]Of all Malagasy populations, only the 22,000 Tambahoaka of the southeast coast are included within a single, common genealogy. Only the Merina and the Sakalava each have a single genealogy linking all members of the nobility.

ethnic distinction. In 1970 Betsileo who migrate to Bara country remain Betsileo. They do not, as they did in pre-Merina days, become Bara. Thus, many of the ethnic units enumerated in the Malagasy census originated as labels for provincial and territorial divisions of the Merina state. Employed also by the French, they were reinforced and today ascribe ethnic status for life.[3]

CULTURAL DIVERSITY AND CULTURAL ADAPTIVE TYPES

Having provided a basis for understanding cultural unity in Madagascar, I shall now examine some of the major differences among Malagasy populations. On the basis of similarities in immediate environment and trade relationships, it is possible to group the twenty Malagasy ethnic units enumerated in the census into a limited number of cultural adaptive types. The typology is based on variables within the local and regional ecosystems in which Malagasy populations participate—on subsistence and exchange patterns of the past and present.

Type I. River valley agriculturalists and ritual specialists (southeast coast)

Five of the ethnic units listed in the census, all located on the southeast coast, are included in this cultural adaptive type. They are Taisaka (325,000),[4] Taimoro (211,000), Zafisoro (43,000), Taifasy (40,000) and Tambahoaka (22,000). Population densities are higher in the river valleys of the southeast coast than in any part of Madagascar except certain areas of Imerina. Manioc, sweet potatoes, beans, an edible arum, and other crops have been cultivated since precolonial days, but the staple is wet rice. Rice is grown in the alluvial soils of river valleys, which are numerous in southeast Madagascar. Though high rainfall renders irrigation unnecessary in most areas of the southeast coast, the agricultural economy involves flood control and terracing techniques. Ethnic group consciousness is emphasized by geographical compartmentalization. Rivers mark the boundaries of the ethnic units. Each named group has a small port in its territory. Under French rule, the southeast coast became a region of cash crops, principally coffee, and of small plantations owned by French creoles from Reunion Island.

---

[3]There have been exceptions in which ethnic designations were determined by environment rather than by political order. The Tanala inhabit the rain forest between the highlands and the east coast. The term Tanala means "people of the forest." Anyone who lives in the forest and practices a Tanala horticultural economy is a Tanala. The common cultural adaptation confers a certain sense of ethnic unity here.

[4]All population figures, unless otherwise indicated, are based on the 1964 census figures as given in Rajemisa-Raolison (1966).

For several centuries, the populations of the southeast coast have participated in regional ecosystems spanning large areas. There is considerable evidence of contact between southeast Madagascar and the East African coast. In addition, one of the coastal populations, the Taimoro, specialized in ritual knowledge and skills which they peddled throughout the island. The Taimoro were the only Malagasy group to possess knowledge of writing (Arabic script used to render Malagasy words) prior to the arrival of the London Missionary Society. For at least 200 years a group of itinerant Taimoro specialists in ritual and esoteric knowledge traveled widely throughout Madagascar. They served as diviners at the courts of Merina, Betsileo and Sakalava rulers, and they brought home cattle and money which they had obtained through application of their ritual knowledge and for instruction in certain skills. Because of heavy population densities which rise to 220 per square kilometer in the Taisaka river valleys, the populations of the southeast coast migrate easily to other parts of the island. About one-fourth of these groups are presently settled outside of their traditional homeland.

Type II. Coastal trade states and political confederations

Included in this type are the Sakalava (360,000) of the west coast, the Betsimisaraka (915,000) of the east coast, and the Tanosy (149,000) of the extreme southeast. In these ethnic units, the basis of both political organization and differential access to wealth and power was control of resources strategic to regional ecosystems which linked Malagasy ethnic units to a number of non-Malagasy economies. City states had arisen on the Malagasy coasts prior to the first arrival of Europeans in Madagascar in 1500. The ruling families of Malagasy port towns oversaw provisioning and the exchange of local products for external imports. Still, the rule of the noble families of such city states did not extend far beyond the port town and its immediate hinterland. At first, European ships merely collected subsistence provisions along the Malagasy coasts. In the latter half of the seventeenth century, however, Europeans began to exchange munitions for Malagasy cattle and slaves. It was this trade which transformed coastal Malagasy society, producing territorial integration of coastal populations beyond the city state.

The earliest, and territorially most extensive and successful, of the trade states, more aptly called political confederations since they contained recognizably separate groups of marine fishermen, freshwater fishermen, pastoralists and horticulturalists

was that of the Sakalava. A group of southern Sakalava, who
were to become the ruling lineage of the Sakalava confederation,
appear to have been the first Malagasy to obtain European
munitions in exchange for Malagasy products. European arms
entered the exchange network in ca. 1660, and by ca. 1700 the
southern Sakalava had extended a loosely organized polity along
most of the west coast. The Sakalava confederation persisted
through the early nineteenth century, when the major port cities
were conquered and annexed by the Merina.

As has been the case with all Malagasy coastal polities, the
authority of the Sakalava rulers appears to have been absolute
only in and immediately around the major port towns. Away
from the coast, the Sakalava are cattle pastoralists. Interior
Sakalava were controlled, tenuously, by the threat and the fact
of raiding parties organized by the nobility and their representatives. Sakalava raiders, seeking war prisoners for European
slavers, also harassed the populations of the western central
highlands until the expanding Merina state built stockades to
protect the highlands from Sakalava marauders.

The slave-firearms trade came later to the east coast than
to the west. The trade state of the Betsimisaraka developed a
half-century later than the Sakalava state, with the introduction
of European firearms on the Malagasy east coast. Its ruling
lineage was also founded on control of the exchange of Malagasy
war prisoners for European munitions. At the time of its max-
imal territorial extent, the Betsimisaraka confederation stretched
along approximately 700 miles of the eastern littoral. In addition to war prisoners, rice, cultivated by the Betsimisaraka
under a swidden regime, and other local products played a role
analagous to that of cattle in the west in the trade with Europeans. As in the west, state control was most effective in the
immediate vicinity of the ports. Interior groups of shifting
horticulturalists were temporarily subdued, only to reassert
their autonomy and be raided again during the century of Betsimisaraka existence as an independent polity, prior to its
conquest by the Merina in the early nineteenth century.

Finally, among the Tanosy of the extreme southeast a city
state and a ruling family had come into existence prior to the
arrival of Europeans, to oversee the exchange of Malagasy and
East African products. European trade items subsequently en-
abled the Tanosy nobility to expand its subject population, but
there was never even the nominal large-scale territorial integration characteristic of the cases just examined.

Type III. Malagasy pastoralists (south and west)

Three of the twenty officially recognized Malagasy ethnic units—Bara (228,000), Mahafaly (91,000) and Tandroy (327,000)— may be placed in this cultural adaptive type along with the non-coastal Sakalava and Tanosy. Madagascar's lowest population densities are encountered in pastoral areas of the south and west Most Malagasy pastoralists are transhumant cattle herders. However, scattered in areas of Bara country where water sources permit, there is cultivation of irrigated rice. Among the Tandroy there is groundwater cultivation of sorghum, maize, manioc and other crops. Elsewhere, the cultivation of these crops depends on rainfall.

During the eighteenth and nineteenth centuries, the Malagasy pastoralists became involved in the slave-munitions exchange network which had produced the coastal trade states, but the effects of a pattern of adaptation which came to be oriented as much towards raiding of neighbors as towards cattle herding was centrifugal, contributing to political fragmentation among these interior populations. Away from the ports, access to European arms was indirect, mediated through exchange with the coastal Malagasy, and no single interior group enjoyed a monopoly on European firearms. In the late nineteenth century, in a population which numbered only 140,000 (Julien, 1908:100) no fewer than forty Bara claimed the status of "king" and competed with one another, in a pattern of constant raiding, for supremacy in Bara land (Nielsen Lund, 1888:443). An equally fragmented polity was characteristic of the Mahafaly and Tandroy, where "kings" were proportionately as ubiquitous and kingship was equally ephemeral (cf. Nielsen Lund, 1888:451). The inability of Sakalava and Tanosy rulers to maintain effective control on a permanent basis over interior populations has been noted above. The sparse population and lack of permanent ties to the land among the pastoral Malagasy was also responsible for failure of Merina military expeditions sent to subdue southern Madagascar. Difficulties in the administration of these mobile cultural adaptations have continued to plague both French and modern Malagasy governments.

Type IV. Swidden cultivators of the tropical forest (eastern escarpment)

Between the east coast and the central highlands is a tropical rain forest which is the homeland of the Tanala (237,000) and, north of them, the interior Betsimisaraka. Subsistence for both populations depends on swidden cultivation of dry rice, maize,

sweet potatoes, manioc and many other crops. The southern
Tanala were never conquered by any other Malagasy population.
During the eighteenth and early nineteenth centuries, in response
to an increased demand for slaves on the east coast, the southern
Tanala carried out raids on their western neighbors, the Betsileo,
and exchanged their prisoners of war on the east coast. They
also preyed on caravans which crossed their country conveying
products to and from the east coast. Access to firearms created
temporary "kings" out of Tanala descent group leaders. Normally dispersed in small villages throughout the forest, members
of several Tanala descent groups assembled on fortified hilltops
when Betsileo and, later, Merina military expeditions invaded
their country. They dispersed again when the military force
withdrew. Tanala "kings" were simply temporary military co-
ordinators and heads of raiding parties whose positions rested
on possession of firearms.

Among the interior Betsimisaraka, swidden cultivators cut
off from the lucrative trade with Europeans by the intervening
coastal populations, a charismatic, "big-man" basis of authority
was characteristic, and deposition of nominal rulers, puppets of
the coastal regime, by influential commoners was frequent.

Type V. Irrigation agriculturalists (central highlands)

It has been stated above that the economy of the Merina
rested on irrigated rice agriculture, long-distance trade and
manufacturing. Though there is a difference in scale, Betsileo
(736,000) and Merina (1,570,000) are placed together in this
cultural adaptive type because of similarities in their agricultural
economies. Both relied for subsistence on wet rice which they
cultivated in irrigated fields. Betsileo outproduce Merina in rice,
but the Merina canal system developed around 1700 in the plain
where Tananarive is located and extended around 1800 is the most
impressive hydraulic achievement in Madagascar. The Betsileo
were incorporated by the Merina state in 1830, and, because of
similarities in their peasant economies, Merina rule over them
was more effective than in other parts of Madagascar. The differences between Merina and Betsileo appear to be quantitative.
Both manufactured certain goods for export to other Malagasy
populations, but the Merina manufacturing and distribution system was much more developed.

Type VI. Mixed pastoralism and horticulture (northeast and north)

With less ethnographic information available, this type is
more tentative than the others. Included are four Malagasy
ethnic units—Tsimihety (428,000), Tankarana (42,000), Sihanaka

(135,000) and Bezanozano (44,000). The homelands of the Sihanaka and the Bezanozano were two of the first additions to the expanding Merina state, and the services and local ecosystems of Sihanaka and Bezanozano became specialized appendages of the Merina economy, supplying labor, pasture land, fish, and basketry products to their overlords. In the absence of archaeological investigation and written documents, their pre-Merina adaptations are difficult to reconstruct, but did, like the Tsimihety and Tankarana, involve cattle herding as well as cultivation of wet and dry varieties of rice and other crops. Tsimihety and Tankarana are remote northern populations traditionally isolated from one another and other Malagasy by natural environmental barriers. Ethnographic knowledge of the Tankarana and historical information about the Tsimihety are necessary before their placement in this type can be confirmed.

CULTURAL ADAPTATION IN POLITICAL ORGANIZATION

I have classified Malagasy ethnic units into six cultural adaptive types on the basis of variables included within local and regional ecosystems. Where data are available, Malagasy populations representing each type will be used to illustrate variation of political organization with respect to adaptive problems associated with each type. Since ethnographic studies have not been carried out among all Malagasy ethnic units, some of the cultural adaptive types are excluded from the following discussion.

Concentration on certain apparent formal similarities rather than attention to differences in actual behavior patterns has led to confusion about comparative political organization in Madagascar. By the nineteenth century most Malagasy ethnic units had developed socioeconomic stratification and political figures whose authority was based on factors other than, and/or in addition to, status over descent group members as elder of that group. The word *mpanjaka* is used by all Malagasy to refer to certain statuses which involve authority over territorial units and the people, kin and nonkin, who reside within them. Those who have described the political organization of different Malagasy ethnic units have stressed the presence of a nobility and have translated mpanjaka as "king" or "chief." Often such characterizations are misleading, as they obscure variations in power and material prerogatives associated with the status of mpanjaka and noble and ignore the ecological and economic factors responsible for these variations.

The Taimoro (Type I)

Among the Taimoro of the densely populated southeast coast the status of "king" or mpanjaka conferred only ritual authority. Ceremonial generosity was associated with the status of noble and chieftainship was a leveling mechanism. Two noble groups among the Taimoro are the Anteoni and the Antalaotra. The former lineage, which furnishes the king, also has the exclusive right of slaughtering sacrificial animals, a service for which its members are compensated. Second in the prestige hierarchy, the Antalaotra were probably the wealthiest Taimoro prior to Merina conquest. From the Antalaotra came diviners, magicians, medicine men, scribes, and scholars versed in the writing of Malagasy with Arabic script. Since at least a century prior to the formation of the Merina state, the Antalaotra have traveled widely in Madagascar, selling charms and inscriptions, spreading knowledge of sand and grain divination, recording descent group genealogies, and serving as advisors to chiefs and kings. Antalaotra were scholarly advisors of the Merina king Radama I until London missionaries replaced them. Antalaotra idol makers and charm consecrators traditionally returned to their native land with herds of cattle, money, and goods garnered during their travels among other Malagasy ethnic units.

What were the perquisites of political office in Taimoro society? The ruling lineage was granted the use of agricultural lands by commoner descent groups. The king's slaves worked his rice fields. A house was maintained for the king in one of the Taimoro towns. The king delegated some of his authority, which was only ritual and judicial, to other members of the Anteoni and Antalaotra groups. These men were known as *randriambe* or "great lords," the literal translation, but it is important to understand that these "great lords" came from precisely those segments of Taimoro society whose wealth in nonlanded resources was greatest. Rather than conferring or protecting any differential access to scarce resources, the office of *randriambe* was associated with ceremonial generosity. The great lords convened the people to public works projects and were supposed to have the support of the community as force behind their orders. However, following the execution of such projects, on occasions when judicial proclamations were made, and in the context of public ceremonials, the great lord was expected to slaughter oxen and to distribute meat and rum. In other parts of Madagascar, as the Malagasy proverb goes, "the king eats the people," but among the Taimoro, the adage is that "the people eat the lord."

The accuracy of this analysis is supported by consideration of certain events which followed Merina conquest of the Taimoro in 1824. The Merina government permitted the Anteoni "king" to retain his title and to receive half of the taxes and tribute collected from his people in the name of the Merina king. The newly introduced prerogatives of Taimoro kingship proved ephemeral and were challenged by a series of commoner revolts between 1850 and 1892. The commoner rebellions were finally suppressed by the Merina in 1892, but the traditional Taimoro nobility lost its elite status. Since 1892 the "privilege" of being a king or great lord has been extended to commoners, among whom it continues to operate as a leveling mechanism. Those who are now elected king or lord hold the office for five to ten years. It is stated by Vianès (Deschamps and Vianès, 1959:51) that these office holders are chosen from among the wealthiest Taimoro, for considerable generosity is expected. Ceremonial expenditures devolving on the king or great lord involve the slaughter of oxen and the distribution of rice, fowls and rum. Since the nineteenth century, the Taimoro have been noted for their proclivity to work for wages outside their homeland. All Malagasy traditionally have stored their wealth in cattle. Among the Taimoro, through the rotating elective offices of king and great lord, cattle are converted from riches of single individuals to the subsistence fund of the folk.

The Bara (Type III)

As has been stated above, in the nineteenth century "kings" or mpanjaka abounded in the pastoral south and west of Madagascar. There is an obvious difference in the meaning of the work mpanjaka when in one case, the Bara, it may be applied to any one of more than forty individuals in a population which numbered 140,000 in 1900, and in another, the Merina, to a single ruler of an ethnic unit whose population was 847,000 in 1900 (Julien, 1908:100) and whose empire covered two-thirds of Madagascar.

As has been noted above, Bara society of the nineteenth century was adapted to raiding. There was never a single Bara mpanjaka. Those Bara who claimed this title appear to have been "big men," leaders of populous descent groups or charismatic individuals who were able to attract clients and supporters on a temporary basis. Their power rested on brute force, their reputations on success in raiding. The benefits involved in associating oneself with such leaders included protection from other Bara groups and a chance to share in the booty of raids.

Most of the Bara mpanjaka claimed to belong to a so-called "royal family," a named descent group found in all parts of Bara land. According to Faublée (1954:105) this family, the Zafimanely, was believed to be associated with certain life spirits of the land. This association was the justification given for a theoretical eminent domain of the noble lineage over the land.

Other commoner descent groups whom Bara oral traditions regard as having lived in Bara territory for as long as the noble group apparently exercised considerable control over the nobles, regularly ousting nobles who displeased them, and installing other members of the royal lineage. The limited nature of royal status among the Bara is revealed by the fact that influential commoner groups presented sacrificial meat and first fruits, signs of allegiance due the mpanjaka among the Merina and Betsileo, to the heads of their own descent groups rather than to the royal descent group.

In the nineteenth century, however, as demands of the regional ecosystem led the Bara towards more and more raiding, the status of Bara mpanjaka appears in some cases actually to have involved considerable authority originating in the mpanjaka's right to admit strangers to lands included within his domain. Faublée (1954:120) asserts that as a mpanjaka's power base grew and his reputation spread, groups would ask for his protection and grants of grazing lands for their herds. As his influence waned or as disputes within the royal family led to segmentation, supporters and clients would disperse and follow other mpanjakas. During the nineteenth century people from adjacent ethnic units— Betsileo from the north, Tanosy from the southeast, and Tandroy from the south—swore allegiance to Bara leaders. One of the ethnographers of the Bara, Jacques Faublée, has argued convincingly that the traditional political organization of the pastoral Bara was based on a structure of segmentary descent groups (1954). During the nineteenth century, European weaponry and demands for war prisoners as slaves transformed the Bara polity into a structure of clientship. However, while royalties rose, fell, and eventually disappeared, the historically prior descent structure endures today.

The Merina (Type V)

The economic foundation of the Merina state has been discussed at length above. There can be no question that "king" is an appropriate rendering of the meaning of the word mpanjaka to the Merina. In 1787, King Andrianampoinimerina, the unifier of Imerina, brought four petty states which had vied for supremacy in the northern highlands during the eighteenth century under centralized rule and established a national capital at Tananarive. The Merina empire, based on the conquest of most of Madagascar, was the work of his son, Radama I. After Radama's death in 1827 a series of queens ruled Madagascar. During their reigns, real power passed to the Merina prime minister, a member of one of the most influential commoner descent groups.

Condominas (1960) has written of the accomplishments of King Andrianampoinimerina, whom he compares to Charlemagne and Napoleon. I shall summarize briefly the major changes effected during his reign which resulted in the creation of the first cohesive and effective Malagasy government. By the end of Andrianampoinimerina's reign in 1810 every villager in Imerina was a member of a nation-state, and the presence of national level institutions in the local community had changed the nature of his daily life. Public works projects, most notably the construction, maintenance and repair of large-scale hydraulic systems, were organized and managed by state personnel. Boundaries of descent group estates were demarcated and clan lands became administrative domains. Access to noble status was restricted as distant members of the royal lineage were divested of all but certain ritual prerogatives. A legal code was formulated and repeatedly modified. To guarantee its operation, administrative, enforcement, and judicial subsystems were differentiated. Taxes, tribute and peasant labor were collected and administered by bureaucrats and nobles. A means of census was devised.

The noble group in Imerina was known as *andriana*. The king's cousins, descendants of previous sovereigns, were granted estates and the right to half of the tribute of the serfs attached to their domains. Throughout the nineteenth century, however, the power of the king grew progressively. Nobles could no longer transmit their domains, which were incorporated into the royal estate. Considerable differences between Merina andriana and commoners in terms of access to wealth and power are still reflected in the life styles and economic positions of contemporary Malagasy. After 64 years of colonial rule, a large percentage of wealthy and influential Merina trace their ancestry to the noble caste of the nineteenth century Merina state.

CONCLUSIONS

The present paper has been an attempt, using the domain of political organization as an example, to demonstrate that despite certain pan-Malagasy homologies in sociocultural forms, there is considerable variation in behavior associated with these forms. I have also attempted to relate this variation to local and regional ecosystemic variables, proposing a set of cultural adaptive types and examining cases of political organization in those types for which data are most abundant. I discussed, for example, several Malagasy ethnic units which conceptualize a status called mpanjaka. Despite the formal similarity, i.e., mpanjaka denotes an office with authority within a territorial unit and over a population including nonkinsmen, there is considerable variation in the behavior of the Taimoro, Bara, and Merina mpanjaka, in the behavior of others to them, and in the material correlates of office.

Previously in the study of political organization and the allocation of power and authority in Madagascar, formal similarities have been emphasized while great material and behavioral differences have been ignored. This is largely the result of the kinds of hypotheses which have oriented research in Madagascar. Thus, the specification of differences in material prerogatives attached to the status of mpanjaka in different Malagasy ethnic units has been subordinated to the study of oral traditions of "noble" groups in each Malagasy society. Data have been gathered by different scholars with the aim of supporting an origin in Mecca or in India for the mpanjakas and real or fictional noble groups among the Taimoro, Tanala, Betsileo, and Bara. Most recently, a combination of oral historical research and eclectic word study has brought the rulers of the Sakalava confederacy from Zimbabwe to western Madagascar (Kent, 1968). The theoretical bias determining such data collection is clear: states do not arise internally and independently; the idea of the state, which must be introduced by outsiders, is a prerequisite to the reality of differential power on a territorial basis.

A cultural adaptive approach, on the other hand, relates political organization to events which have influenced the Malagasy in Madagascar itself. In the Sakalava case, given a Malagasy population on the west coast, the existence of natural harbors, European slave ships, and the possibility of exchanging war captives for rifles, the development of a state was inevitable. Given limited possibilities for agriculture among the Bara, the mobility associated with a pastoral economy, a European demand for slaves and cattle, and a ready supply of European ammunition, 40 kings vying for the allegiance of 140,000 people is an expectable adaptive response. In the case of the Taimoro, given a limited geographical area bounded on the east by the ocean, on the west by an escarpment and tropical forest, and on the north and south by rivers and equally armed populations, and given a ruling class whose organizational and managerial role in the local economy was limited and whose aspirations, if any, for power could only be realized elsewhere, the absence of major stratification and absolute kingship in Taimoro society could be predicted.

During the 2000 years they have lived on their island, the Malagasy have not simply been retaining ancestral cultural features and borrowing traits and institutions in an automatic fashion. They have been concerned with problems of wresting a living from the land, and they have met modifications in physical, biotic and intercultural environments with a related series of cultural adaptive responses.

SUMMARY COMMENTS: EVOLUTIONARY TRENDS IN SOCIAL EXCHANGE AND INTERACTION

Kent V. Flannery

TO summarize the contents of this symposium volume is a seemingly impossible task, since the range of topics covered is so great and the approaches of the various authors so disparate. Instead, I will comment on one aspect of exchange which emerges from the seven papers under consideration, and which clearly has some universal implications: that is, the evolutionary aspect of social exchange. For these papers, which run a gamut from hunting and gathering societies through egalitarian cultivators to stratified nation-states, reinforce the notion that specific types of exchange and interaction are characteristic of various levels of sociocultural complexity.

Yengoyan's paper makes a useful distinction between two types of intergroup rituals: the "unscheduled," time-independent communal rituals of low-density hunters and gatherers, and the "scheduled," time-dependent or calendric rituals of higher-density populations like Ford's Pueblo Indians. Ritual interaction among scattered groups of Australian hunter-gatherers is *ad hoc*, occurring only "under favorable environmental conditions which permit local groups to cluster for several days." This interaction, to which Yengoyan assigns the adaptive function of maintaining solidarity under conditions of highly dispersed population, cannot be sustained on a scheduled basis because of the unreliability of food and water; the ritual is triggered by unpredictable moments of abundance.

Among successful food-producers, however, where harvests occur at predictable times of the year, there are time-dependent rituals which "follow agricultural, religious, or political calendars with marked temporal regularity." I would agree that population density and resource availability might help to explain the absence of such scheduled interaction in hunting groups and its frequency among sedentary agriculturalists, but I do not believe that it is necessarily paralleled by the Durkheimian distinction ("mechanical" versus "organic" solidarity) which Yengoyan sees.

Indeed, Ford's paper suggests that the interacting Tewa and Comanche are even more "functionally differentiated" than Yengoyan's aborigine bands.

Frison's paper carries the theme of dispersal and recombination into the realm of the High Plains bison hunter. Here the Indians spent the winter at scattered, single-family campsites, but began to converge in late summer or early fall for the communal bison slaughter, which involved drives, jumps, or traps. A minimum of 30 participants were needed for a drive, and the biggest bison-jump sites may have required 120 to 140 persons. At least one large trap site had a ceremonial structure for "shamanistic" activity connected with the bison kills; again, therefore, we see the evidence for specific kinds of ceremonialism which occur only when normally scattered groups have temporarily coalesced. The exact time and day of the ceremonial interaction is *ad hoc*, as with Yengoyan's aborigines, and yet it should have been possible to predict that it would occur sometime in the late summer or early fall, based on the availability of bison. Among the bison hunters, as among the Australian hunters, we sense also that the ceremonial interaction is among the far-flung components of a single ethnic group—not between strangers and enemies, as in the Tewa-Comanche example to be discussed below.

Ford's paper deals with a sedentary Pueblo Indian society, whose population density and community size are considerably greater than those of either the Australians or Plains bison hunters. It is still an unstratified society, however, where integration is accomplished by a very strong ritual system in lieu of a strong hierarchical polity. Within the ethnic group, village subdivisions known as sodalities (medicine societies, clown societies, etc.), who take turns sponsoring different kinds of communal rituals, have replaced the "dispersing and coalescing" local groups seen among hunters; now "coalescence" comes on a more massive, scheduled, time-dependent basis. Their elaborate calendric rituals require esoteric goods, many of which come from great distances away. To procure such goods they engage in long-distance exchange with ethnic groups of completely different language, ethnic background, and life style—unfriendly Comanches who may "trade today and kill tomorrow." Such regional trade, as Ford points out, is "a form of foreign relations." It also is usually *ad hoc*, unscheduled, and time-independent, in contrast to the ritual interactions *within* the Tewa pueblos.

Here Ford introduces the concept of the "trade partner," an institution which is well-developed at the level of the sedentary egalitarian tribe. Tewa families have Jicarilla Apache trade partners, who in several instances have been "inherited" for at least three generations within the same family. Tewa relations with the more hostile Comanche, however, were extremely tenuous since trade partnerships did not exist between the two tribes; the Tewa needed the goodwill of the Comanche band leader before they could venture into the latter's territory and return with the bison heads and hides so important in the "intramural" rituals within the Tewa community.

While scheduled ceremonial interaction between Tewa sodalities circulated goods and services among members of the community, their *ad hoc* foreign relations with neighboring nomadic groups were so important, it appears, that certain goods derived from the latter always managed to get "used up" in ritual so there would be continued need for them. Finally, in anticipation of what is to come, we should add that Tewa foreign trade was still conducted by Indian farmers, who were not "professional traders" in any sense—although some of them functioned as "middle men" on occasion.

Ford's paper provides a convenient model for interpreting some of Struever and Houart's archaeological data. The Middle Woodland Indians discussed by Struever and Houart also seem to have been integrated by very strong ritual systems in which esoteric goods circulated on an immense scale and were "used up" in such a way that more would have to be sought. Copper, mica, and obsidian, carried far from their source areas, were temporarily or permanently taken out of circulation by burial or caching.

Struever and Houart stress that many "functionally different" groups (to use Yengoyan's term)—differing presumably on ethnic, political, economic, and linguistic grounds—participated in the exchanges of such material. The authors call on Joseph Caldwell's term, "the interaction sphere," to describe the interregional network which linked Ohio farmer-hunters, Illinois food-collectors, and Indiana mound-builders into a complex and far-flung exchange system. In the interaction sphere, raw materials, stylistic concepts, and finished goods (some communicating status, others serving as paraphernalia in the ritual reinforcement of status) circulated among several different regional populations, each of which bears analogy to Ford's Tewa. It is Struever and Houart's contention that the archaeologically observable ritual activity "was all part of a *seasonal* [my emphasis] pattern of ceremonial and economic functions which served to distribute interaction sphere goods coming into or leaving the locality." If so, the internal exchange of goods may have been seasonally scheduled and time-dependent like many pueblo ceremonies—possibly our first glimpse in this volume of a level of sociopolitical integration in which interethnic group ritual is so scheduled. But beyond the interaction sphere, in areas like Yellowstone Park where the traded obsidian came from, there must have been hunting and gathering bands who carried on exchange with the Middle Woodland Indians in the same semihostile, *ad hoc* way that the Comanche traded with the Tewa.

Thus the Middle Woodland picture given by Struever and Houart suggests (1) intragroup or sodality-sponsored rituals, probably time-dependent, in which stylistic concepts played a great role; (2) intergroup exchange, perhaps time-dependent, between different Middle Woodland polities who had different economies but participated in the same interaction sphere; and (3) presumably *ad hoc* exchanges between the interaction sphere and groups external to it, who controlled some of the exotic raw materials. Finally, Struever and Houart introduce a concept which is to play a role in all higher levels of sociopolitical organization site hierarchy. In the Middle Woodland exchange network, there are "interaction sphere centers" which serve as "primary nodes" and contain most of the exotic trade goods; regional centers, which are smaller and more common; and local centers, which are still smaller and most common, receiving less of the trade goods.

It is not clear to what extent the Middle Woodland Indians might have had a more "ranked" or less egalitarian society than the Tewa, but with Wright's Near Eastern peoples we move up to the level of clearly stratified societies. Wright shows how archaeologists can use quantitative measures of exotic and local materials to study import and export in archaic states, to judge fluctuations in the volume of transport, and to measure changes in the value of imports through time. Such studies can also help in considering the problem of whether increased or decreased trade causes, is caused by, or has no relationship to changes in political organization.

In this paper, Wright utilizes the concepts of site hierarchy and of the site's role as a node in an exchange network, already discussed by Struever and Houart. He further introduces two useful assumptions used by locational geographers: (1) that the value of a commodity is a function of transport distance from

the source, and (2) that the volume of a commodity moving
through a point is a function of the population served by that
part of the network beyond that point. In Wright's paper we see
the rise, decline, and renaissance of Tepe Farukhabad as a node
in a prehistoric Near Eastern exchange network, and we learn
that the political climate rather than distance to raw material
is probably the main determinant of whether a given town is a
primary center, regional center, or local center in Struever and
Houart's terms. And Wright's paper touches on "central places"—
towns whose primary function is to act as nodes for interaction
between differing local groups—which are perhaps present to a
degree in simpler societies, but more highly developed in archaic
states.

Both Benedict and Kottak bring us up to the level of more
recent states in the "third world." Benedict's paper, dealing
with market exchange in modern Turkey, shows us what may
happen in the later developmental stages of a network of primary, secondary, and tertiary nodes. As rural affluence increases,
clients who formerly supported the "local" and "regional" centers begin to by-pass them, going directly to the "central place"
or "interaction sphere center." Stripped of their sustaining
population, the secondary nodes begin to decline in importance;
accompanying the decline of the regional center is an emigration
of merchants who become the itinerant professional marketers of
the primary node. The rise of this class of traders signals a
way-station along the evolutionary route from a rural-agricultural
to an urban-capitalist economy—the substitution of services for
agriculture, the mass use of unskilled labor instead of capital
in the performance of distribution. For Benedict, market economy is thus a transitional form, reflecting widespread poverty
and surplus labor rather than "progress," and probably destined
in the future to be replaced by a modern Western type of economy. And his itinerant marketers are our first clear glimpse
in this volume of the evolution of a full-time trader class.

Kottak's paper touches on another side of the evolving state,
the way it interacts with other states on the one hand and with
less-developed chiefdoms on the other. In preparation for this,
he divides Madagascar into a series of "cultural adaptive types"
based on differences in subsistence and exchange. So massive
was the exchange that certain coastal areas gave rise to "trade
states" which functioned as "middle men" or engaged in exchanges of slaves and munitions with other states. Here is a
situation in which a "node" can rise to primary status, supported primarily by "rakeoffs" from its administration of the

flow of goods and services passing through it to other nodes. This, at least, was their interaction with other states; with chiefdoms, on a lower level of sociocultural integration, their interaction was far more predatory. The coastal states raided neighboring chiefdoms to obtain slaves, exchanging these with other states to obtain weapons. In turn, the weapons made raiding easier, and allowed the descent group leaders to back up claims of "kingship."

The evolution of exchange and interaction, seen in dim outline in this volume of collected papers, is therefore as follows. It begins among hunters and gatherers in areas of low population density and meager, seasonally unpredictable resources, taking the form of *ad hoc* or time-independent ritual which brings together scattered segments of the same ethnic group. Among higher density, sedentary tribespeople, capable of producing a ceremonial surplus, intragroup ritual interaction evolves into a time-dependent, scheduled series of ceremonies, whose sponsorship is rotated by artificial subgroups or sodalities within the group. In addition, such tribespeople engage in *ad hoc*, unscheduled, and sometimes very dangerous longer-distance exchange with people who are ethnically and linguistically different. By the time "ranked" societies appear, and perhaps even earlier, some of this "foreign relations" trade has become so important in the social and ceremonial system that certain villages or towns have emerged as primary or secondary "nodes" in a formalized exchange network.

As chiefdoms or ranked societies evolved into states, ritual rotation of sodality-sponsored ceremonies probably lessened in importance, but did not disappear. Foreign trade, formerly *ad hoc* and erratic, became a massive flow of goods, so continuous that certain nodes in the network could support bureaucracies merely on their "overhead" from through-flow. A professional merchant class was recruited from the ranks of unskilled emigrants from declining secondary and tertiary nodes. Some states became so powerful that their main form of interaction with lesser polities came to be *ad hoc* predation.

This is as far as the evolution can be traced in this symposium; now let me attempt to summarize it in three sentences. If human ecosystems are viewed as systems of exchanges of matter, energy, and information between human populations and their effective environment, all the "social exchange and interaction" described in this volume contributes heavily to the "information" component, as Wilmsen points out in his introduction. Virtually every evolutionary change amounts to (1) the assignment of "scheduled" status to a previously *ad hoc* excharge of information about social distance and relationships between two or more human groups, and (2) the addition of a new *ad hoc* exchange which collects information about still more divergent groups. Moreover, at each evolutionary step, a new institution for information-processing is added—sodalities, trade partners, middle men, central places, and finally professional merchants, to mention only a few. It might provide a great deal of unexpected fun if future studies used such exchange as a window into each society's explosively evolving ability to collect and process information about neighboring societies.

REFERENCES

Abel, Annie Heloise, ed.
    1913   The Journal of John Greiner. Old Sante Fe 3:189-242.
    1915   The Official Correspondence of James S. Calhoun while Indian Agent at Santa Fe and Superintendent of Indian Affairs in New Mexico. Government Printing Office. Washington.

Adams, Eleanor B. and Fray Angelico Chavez, eds.
    1956   The Missions of New Mexico, 1776. The University of New Mexico Press. Albuquerque.

Baker, Frank C., James B. Griffin, Richard G. Morgan, Georg K. Neumann and J. L. B. Taylor
    1941   Contribution to the Archeology of the Illinois River Valley. American Philosophical Society, Transactions Vol. 32, Pt. 1. Philadelphia.

Bancroft, H. H.
    1889   The Works of H. H. Bancroft, Vol. 17, History of Arizona and New Mexico: 1530-1888. The History Company. San Francisco.

Bandelier, A. F.
    1890   Final Report of Investigations Among the Indians of the Southwestern United States, Carried on Mainly in the Years from 1880 to 1885, Part I. Papers of the Archaeological Institute of America. American Series III.

Barnum, H. G.
    1966   Market Centers and Hinterlands in Baden-Württemberg. Department of Geography Research Paper No. 103. University of Chicago. Chicago.

Bauer, P. T. and B. S. Yamey
    1951   Economic Progress and Occupational Distribution. Economic Journal 61(244):741-55.

Belshaw, C. S.
    1965   Traditional Exchange and Modern Markets. Prentice-Hall, Inc. New Jersey.

Bentzen, Raymon C.
    1961   The Powers-Yonkee Bison Trap, 24 PR 5. Report of Sheridan Chapter, Wyoming Archaeological Society. Sheridan, Wyoming.

1963 The Bentzen-Little Bald Mountain Site. Plains Anthropologist Vol. 8, No. 19:41-51. Lincoln.

Bohannan, P. and G. Dalton
1965 Markets in Africa. Doubleday & Company, Inc. New York.

Brown, James, ed.
1968 Hopewell and Woodland Site Archaeology in Illinois. Illinois Archaeological Survey, Bulletin 6. Urbana.

Caldwell, Joseph R.
1964 Interaction Spheres in Prehistory. In: Hopewellian Studies. Joseph R. Caldwell and Robert L. Hall, eds. Illinois State Museum, Scientific Papers Vol. 12, No. 6:133-43.

Clark, C.
1951 The Conditions of Economic Progress. Macmillan & Company, Ltd. London.

Cole, Fay-Cooper, and Thorne Deuel
1937 Rediscovering Illinois. University of Chicago Press. Chicago

Condominas, Georges
1960 Fokon'olona et Collectivités Rurales en Imerina. Éditions Berger-Levrault. Paris.

Conduché, R.
1960 Les Commerces non Sédantaires dans le Distribution Commerciale Marches et Tournées. La Vie Urbaine No. 3:173-224, No. 4:299-314.

Curr, Edward M.
1886-1887 The Australian Race. John Ferres. Melbourne.

Curtis, Edward S.
1926 The North American Indian. Vol. 17. Plimpton Press. Norwood.

Dalton, George
1967 Tribal and Peasant Economies: Readings in Economic Anthropology. Natural History Press. Garden City.

Dandouau, A. and G. S. Chapus
1952 Histoire des Populations de Madagascar. Larose. Paris.

Del Monte, Monte
n.d. A Style Analysis of Hopewell Ceramics in the Great Lakes Area. Unpublished manuscript on file at the Department of Anthropology, Northwestern University. Evanston.

Deschamps, Hubert
1960 Histoire de Madagascar. Éditions Berger-Levrault. Paris.

REFERENCES

Deschamps, Hubert and Suzanne Vianès
    1959   Les Malgaches du Sud-Est. Presses Universitaires de France. Paris.

Dewey, A. G.
    1962   Peasant Marketing in Java. The Free Press of Glencoe, Inc. New York.

DiPeso, Charles C.
    1968   Casas Grandes and the Gran Chichimeca. Museum of New Mexico Press. Santa Fe.

Donaldson, Thomas
    1893   Moqui Pueblo Indians of Arizona and Pueblo Indians of New Mexico. Eleventh Census of the United States, Extra Census Bulletin, pp. 75-97.

Dozier, Edward P.
    1960   The Pueblos of the Southwestern United States. Journal of the Royal Anthropological Institute 90:146-60.
    1961   Rio Grande Pueblos. In: Perspectives in American Indian Culture Change. Edward H. Spicer, ed. The University of Chicago Press. Chicago.
    1970   The Pueblo Indians of North America. Holt, Rinehart and Winston, Inc. New York.

Faublée, Jacques
    1954   La Cohésion des Sociétés Bara. Presses Universitaires de France, Paris.

Fecht, William G.
    1955   Mound Explorations at Meppen, Illinois. Central States Archeological Journal Vol. 2, No. 1:29-34.

Fischer, A. G. B.
    1945   Economic Progress and Social Security. Macmillan & Company, Ltd. London.

Flacourt, Etienne de
    1661   Histoire de la Grande Île de Madagascar. In: Collection des Ouvrages Anciens Concernant Madagascar. A. Grandidier et al., eds. Union Coloniale IX:1-426. Paris.

Fowke, Gerard
    1905   The Montezuma Mounds. Missouri Historical Society, Collections Vol. 2, No. 5:1-16.

Fried, Morton
    1959   On the Evolution of Social Stratification and the State. In: Culture in History. Stanley Diamond, ed. Columbia University Press. New York.

Frison, George C.
  1965   Spring Creek Cave, Wyoming. American Antiquity Vol. 31, No. 1:81-94. Salt Lake.
  1967a Archaeological Evidence of the Crow Indians in Northern Wyoming: A Study of a Late Prehistoric Period Buffalo Economy. Ph.D. dissertation, University of Michigan, Ann Arbor.
  1967b The Piney Creek Sites, Wyoming. University of Wyoming Publications Vol. 33, No. 1. Laramie.
  1968a Site 48 SH 312: An Early Middle Period Bison Kill in the Powder River Basin of Wyoming. Plains Anthropologist Vol. 13, No. 39:31-39. Lincoln.
  1968b Daugherty Cave, Wyoming. Plains Anthropologist Vol. 13, No. 42:253-95. Lawrence.
  1970   The Kobold Site, 24 BH 406: A Post-Altithermal Record of Buffalo-Jumping for the Northwestern Plains. Plains Anthropologist Vol. 15, No. 47:1-35. Lawrence.
  1971   The Bison Pound in Northwestern Plains Prehistory. American Antiquity Vol. 36, No. 1:77-91. Salt Lake City.

Frison, George C. and Marion Huseas
  1968   Leigh Cave, Wyoming: Site 48 WA 304. The Wyoming Archaeologist Vol. 11, No. 3:20-33. Cheyenne.

Goldstein, Lynne
  n.d.   An Analysis of Plummets in the Lower Illinois Valley. Unpublished manuscript.

Goodonough, Ward
  1955   A Problem in Malayo-Polynesian Social Organization. American Anthropologist 57:71-83.

Grandidier, A. et al.
  1920   Collection des Ouvrages Anciens Concernant Madagascar IX. Union Coloniale. Paris.

Griffin, James B., A. A. Gordus and G. A. Wright
  1969   Identification of the Sources of Hopewellian Obsidian in the Middle West. American Antiquity Vol. 34, No. 1:1-22.

Gulliver, P. H.
  1955   The Family Herds: A Study of Two Pastoral Peoples in East Africa, the Jie and the Turkana. Humanities Press. New York.

Harrington, John P.
  1916   The Ethnogeography of the Tewa Indians. Bureau of American Ethnology, Annual Report No. 29:29-618.

Henderson, John G.
  1884   Aboriginal Remains Near Naples, Illinois. Smithsonian Institution, Annual Report (for 1882):686-721.

REFERENCES

Hesselberth, Charles
- 1945 An Ohio Type Hopewell Ceremonial Mound. Illinois State Archaeological Society Journal Vol. 3, No. 1:18-20.
- 1946 Notes on the Ogden-Fettie Mounds. Illinois State Archaeological Society Journal Vol. 4, No. 1:9-13.

Hodge, F. W.
- 1907 The Narrative of the Expedition of Coronado by Pedro de Castenada. In: Spanish Explorers in the Southern United States, 1528-1543. F. W. Hodge and T. H. Lewis, eds. Charles Scribner's Sons. New York.

Husted, Wilfred
- 1969 Big Horn Canyon Archaeology. Smithsonian Institution, River Basin Survey Publication No. 12. Lincoln.

Julien, Gustave
- 1908 Institutions Politiques et Sociales de Madagascar, Vol. I. E. Guilmoto. Paris.

Kaplan, D.
- 1965 The Mexican Marketplace Then and Now. In: Essays in Economic Anthropology. J. Helm, ed. Proceedings of the American Ethnological Society. University of Washington Press. Seattle.

Kenner, Charles L.
- 1969 A History of New Mexico—Plains Indian Relations. University of Oklahoma Press. Norman.

Kent, Raymond
- 1968 Madagascar and Africa, II: The Sakalava, Maroserana, Dady and Tromba before 1700. Journal of African History 9 (4): 517-46.

Lange, Charles H.
- 1959 Cochiti. University of Texas Press. Austin.

Lange, Charles H. and Carroll L. Riley, eds.
- 1966 The Southwestern Journals of Adolf F. Bandelier 1880-1882. The University of New Mexico Press. Albuquerque.

LeClair, Edward E., Jr. and Harold K. Schneider
- 1968 Economic Anthropology: Readings in Theory and Analysis. Holt, Rinehart and Winston. New York.

Lewis, Edwin C.
- 1874 Pueblo Indian Agency. U. S. Office of Indian Affairs. Annual Report of the Commissioner of Indian Affairs to the Secretary of the Interior for the Year 1874:308-10.

Malinowski, Bronislaw
- 1922 Argonauts of the Western Pacific. Rutledge and Kegan Paul. London.

Mauss, Marcel
    1954   The Gift: Forms and Function of Exchange in Archaic Society. Free Press. New York.

McAdams, William C.
    1884   Mounds of the Mississippi Bottom, Illinois. Smithsonian Institution, Annual Report (for 1882):684-86.
    1887   Records of Ancient Races in the Mississippi Valley. C. R. Barns Publishing Company. St. Louis.

McGregor, John C.
    1952   The Havana Site. In: Hopewellian Communities in Illinois. Thorne Deuel, ed. Illinois State Museum Scientific Papers Vol. 5. Springfield.

McInnes, W.
    1964   A Conceptual Approach to Marketing. In: Theory in Marketing. Second series. R. Cox et al., eds. R. D. Irwin, Inc. Homewood, Illinois.

McKern, W. C.
    1931   A Wisconsin Variant of the Hopewell Culture. Public Museum of the City of Milwaukee Bulletin Vol. 10, No. 2. Milwaukee.

Medicine Crow, Joe
    1962a   Panel Discussion on Buffalo Jumps. In: Symposium on Buffalo Jumps. Montana Archaeological Society Memoir No. 1. Missoula.
    1962b   Crow Indian Buffalo Legends. In: Symposium on Buffalo Jumps. Montana Archaeological Society Memoir No. 1. Missoula.

Meggitt, M. J.
    1964a   Indigenous Forms of Government among the Australian Aborigines. Bijdragen tot de Taal-, Land-, en Volkenkunde 120:163-80.
    1964b   Pre-industrial Man in the Tropical Environment: Aboriginal Food-gatherers of Tropical Australia. Proceedings and Papers of the Ninth Technical Meeting I.U.C.N., Nairobi, Kenya, 1963. International Union for the Conservation of Natural Resources. Morges (Vaud), Switzerland.

Meyers, J. Thomas
    n.d.   A Preliminary Assessment of Chert Availability in the Lower Illinois Valley. Illinois State Museum, Illinois Valley Archeological Program, Research Papers No. 2.

Mikesell, M.
    1958   The Role of Tribal Markets in Morocco. Geographical Review 48(4):494-511.

REFERENCES

Mills, William C.
    1922   Exploration of the Mound City Group. Ohio Archaeological and Historical Society Quarterly Vol. 31, No. 4. Columbus.

Mintz, S. W.
    1956   The Role of the Middleman in the Internal Distribution System of a Caribbean Peasant Economy. Human Organization 15(2):18-23.

Moorehead, Warren
    1922   The Hopewell Mound Group of Ohio. Field Museum of Natural History Anthropological Series Vol. 6, No. 5. Chicago.

Nash, M.
    1966   Primitive and Peasant Economic Systems. Chandler Publishing Company. San Francisco.

Nickerson, William B.
    1912   The Burial Mounds at Albany, Illinois. Records of the Past Vol. 11:69-81.

Nielsen Lund, J.
    1888   Travels and Perils among the Wild Tribes in the South of Madagascar. Antananarivo Annual Vol. III, Pt. IV:440-56.

Ortiz, Alfonso
    1965   Dual Organization as an Operational Concept in the Pueblo Southwest. Ethnology 4 (4):389-96.
    1969   The Tewa World. The University of Chicago Press. Chicago.

Parsons, Elsie Clews
    1929   The Social Organization of the Tewa of New Mexico. Memoirs of the American Anthropological Association No. 36.
    1939   Pueblo Indian Relgion. The University of Chicago Press. Chicago.

Perino, Gregory
    1961   Tentative Classification of Plummets in the Lower Illinois River Valley. Central States Archaeological Journal Vol. 8, No. 2:43-56.
    1966a   A Preliminary Report on the Peisker Site: Part I—The Early Woodland Occupation. Central States Archaeological Journal Vol. 13, No. 2:47-50.
    1966b   A Preliminary Report on the Peisker Site: Part II—The Havana Occupation. Central States Archaeological Journal Vol. 13, No. 3:84-89.
    1968   The Pete Klunk Mound Group, Calhoun County, Illinois: The Archaic and Hopewell Occupations. *In*: Hopewell and Woodland Site Archeology in Illinois. James A. Brown, ed. Illinois Archeological Survey, Bulletin 6:9-124. Urbana.
    n.d.a   Hopewellian Sites in Western Illinois. Unpublished manuscript.
    n.d.b   Meppen Mound Group. Unpublished manuscript.

Pope, Nathaniel
　1872　Office of Superintendent of Indian Affairs. U. S. Office of Indian Affairs. Annual Report of the Commissioner of Indian Affairs to the Secretary of the Interior for the Year 1872 (49):295-302.

Pratt, W. H.
　1876　Report of Explorations of the Ancient Mounds at Albany, Whiteside County, Illinois. Davenport Academy of Natural Sciences, Proceedings Vol. 1, No. 1:99-104.

Preston, L. E.
　1968　The Commercial Sector and Economic Development. *In*: Markets and Marketing in Developing Economies. R. Moyer and S. C. Hollander, eds. R. D. Irwin, Inc. Homewood, Illinois.

Prufer, Olaf
　1961　Prehistoric Hopewell Meteorite Collecting: Context and Implications. Ohio Journal of Science Vol. 61:341-52.
　1964　The Hopewell Complex of Ohio. *In*: Hopewellian Studies. Joseph R. Caldwell and Robert L. Hall, eds. Illinois State Museum Scientific Papers Vol. 12, No. 2:35-83.

Prufer, Olaf (and others)
　1965　The McGraw Site: A Study in Hopewellian Dynamics. Cleveland Museum of Natural History Scientific Publications Vol. 4, No. 1. Cleveland.

Rackerby, Frank
　1969　Preliminary Report on the Macoupin Site: A Lower Illinois Valley Middle Woodland Settlement. Unpublished paper presented at the Annual Meeting of the Society for American Archeology. Milwaukee.
　1970　Exchange Systems and the Hopewell Interaction Sphere. Unpublished paper presented at the Annual Meeting of the Society for American Archeology. Mexico City.

Rajemisa-Raolison, Régis
　1966　Dictionnaire Historique et Géographique de Madagascar. Fianarantsoa, Centre de Formation Pédagogique.

Renfrew, Colin, J. E. Dixon, and J. R. Cann
　1969　Further Analysis of Near Eastern Obsidians. Proceedings of the Prehistoric Society for 1968 Vol. XXXIV:319-31.

Sahlins, Marshall
　1958　Social Stratification in Polynesia. University of Washington Press. Seattle.
　1963　Poor Man, Rich Man, Big-Man, Chief: Political Types in Melanesia and Polynesia. Comparative Studies in Society and History 5 (3):285-303.

REFERENCES

 1965 On the Sociology of Primitive Exchange. *In*: The Relevance of Models for Social Anthropology. Michael Banton, ed. Association of Social Anthropologists Monographs 1:139-236.
 1968 Tribesmen. Prentice-Hall, Inc. Englewood Cliffs.

Sahlins, Marshall and Elman Service
 1960 Evolution and Culture. The University of Michigan Press. Ann Arbor.

Schroeder, Albert H.
 1965 Unregulated Diffusion from Mexico into the Southwest Prior to A.D. 700. American Antiquity 30(3):297-309.

Service, Elman
 1962 Primitive Social Organization: an Evolutionary Account. Random House. New York.

Shaeffer, Claude E.
 1962 The Bison Drive of the Blackfeet Indians. *In*: Symposium on Buffalo Jumps. Montana Archaeological Society Memoir No. 1. Missoula.

Shetrone, Henry C.
 1926 Exploration of the Hopewell Group of Prehistoric Earthworks. Ohio Archaeological and Historical Society Quarterly Vol. 35, No. 1. Columbus.

Shetrone, Henry C. and Emerson F. Greenman
 1931 Explorations of the Seip Group of Prehistoric Earthworks. Ohio Archaeological and Historical Society Quarterly Vol. 40, No. 3:349-509. Columbus.

Singer, Philip and Daniel E. DeSole
 1967 The Australian Subincision Ceremony Reconsidered: Vaginal Envy or Kangaroo Bifid Penis Envy. American Anthropologist 69:355-58.

Spencer, Robert
 1959 The North Alaskan Eskimo: A Study in Ecology and Society. Bureau of American Ethnology Bulletin 171. Washington.

Squier, Ephraim G. and Edwin H. Davis
 1848 Ancient Monuments of the Mississippi Valley. Smithsonian Institution. Contributions to Knowledge Vol. 1. Washington.

Starr, S. F.
 1960 The Archaeology of Hamilton County, Ohio. Cincinnati Museum of Natural History Journal Vol. 23, No. 1. Cincinnati.

Steward, Julian
 1955 Theory of Culture Change. University of Illinois Press. Urbana.

Steward, Julian et al.
   1956   The People of Puerto Rico: a Study in Social Anthropology. University of Illinois Press. Urbana.

Stine, J. H.
   1962   Temporal Aspects of Tertiary Production Elements in Korea. In: Urban Systems and Economic Development. F. R. Pitts, ed. University of Oregon. Eugene.

Struever, Stuart
   1960   The Kamp Mound Group and a Hopewell Mortuary Complex in the Lower Illinois Valley. Unpublished Master's thesis, Department of Anthropology, Northwestern University. Evanston.
   1964   The Hopewell Interaction Sphere in Riverine-Western Great Lakes Culture History. In: Hopewellian Studies. Joseph R. Caldwell and Robert L. Hall, eds. Illinois State Museum Scientific Papers Vol. 12, No. 3:85-106.
   1965   Middle Woodland Culture History in the Great Lakes-Riverine Area. American Antiquity Vol. 31, No. 2:211-23.
   1968   A Re-Examination of Hopewell in Eastern North America. Unpublished Ph.D. dissertation, Department of Anthropology, University of Chicago.

Tindale, Norman B.
   1940   Results of the Harvard-Adelaide Universities Anthropological Expedition, 1938-1939: Distribution of Australian Aboriginal Tribes: A Field Survey. Transactions of the Royal Society of South Australia 64:140-231.

Thomas, Alfred Barnaby
   1940   The Plains Indians and New Mexico, 1751-1778. University of New Mexico Press. Albuquerque.

Thomas, Cyrus
   1894   Report of the Mound Explorations of the Bureau of Ethnology. Bureau of Ethnology, 12th Annual Report (J. W. Powell).

Tiffany, A. S.
   1876   Report on the Results of the Excursion to Albany, Illinois. Davenport Academy of Sciences, Proceedings Vol. 1:104-06.

Vérin, Pierre, Conrad Kottak, and Peter Gorlin
   1970   The Glottochronology of Malagasy Speech Communities. Oceanic Linguistics. In press.

Walton, Clyde C., ed., Phyllis E. Connolly and Melvin L. Fowler
   1962   John Francis Synder: Selected Writings. Illinois State Historical Society. Springfield.

Wedel, Waldo R., W. M. Husted and J. H. Moss
   1968   Mummy Cave: Prehistoric Record from Rocky Mountains of Wyoming. Science Vol. 160:184-86. Washington.

REFERENCES

White, Leslie A.
    1935   The Pueblo of Santo Domingo, New Mexico. Memoirs of the American Anthropological Association. No. 43.

Willoughby, Charles C. and Earnest A. Hooton
    1922   The Turner Group of Earthworks, Hamilton County, Ohio. Peabody Museum of Archaeology and Ethnology Vol. 8, No. 3. Cambridge.

Winters, Howard D.
    1964   The Hopewellian Interaction Sphere: A Reappraisal. Unpublished paper presented at the 29th Annual Meeting of the Society for American Archaeology. Chapel Hill.

    1968   Value Systems and Trade Cycles of the Late Archaic in the Midwest. *In*: New Perspectives in Archeology. Sally R. and Lewis R. Binford, eds. Aldine. Chicago.

Yengoyan, Aram A.
    1968*a*   Demographic and Ecological Influences on Aboriginal Australian Marriage Sections. *In*: Man the Hunter. R. Lee and I. DeVore, eds. Aldine. Chicago.
    1968*b*   Australian Section Systems—Demographic Components and Interactional Similarities with the Kung Bushmen. Proceedings of the VIIIth International Congress of Anthropological and Ethnological Sciences 3:256-60. Tokyo.

www.ingramcontent.com/pod-product-compliance
Lightning Source LLC
Jackson TN
JSHW070313120426
100741JS00007B/48